Super Easy

KETO AIR FRYER

COOKBOOK FOR

BEGINNERS

QUICK AND TASTY LOW-CARB AIR FRYER MEALS FOR WEIGHT LOSS AND HEALTHY LIFESTYLE | 8-WEEK MEAL PLAN

CLARISSA PATTON

WARNING-DISCLAIMER:

The purpose of this book is to educate and entertain. The author or publisher does not guarantee that anyone following the techniques, suggestions, tips, ideas, or strategies will become successful. The author and publisher shall have neither liability nor responsibility to anyone with respect to any loss or damage caused, or alleged to be caused, directly or indirectly, by the information contained in this book.

TABLE OF CONTENTS

When I first embarked on my ketogenic journey five years ago, I found myself standing in my kitchen, staring at a greasy skillet and longing for the crispy, crunchy textures I'd given up in pursuit of better health. Like many of you, I'd heard the promises of the keto diet—enhanced mental clarity, sustained energy, and yes, effective weight management. But I struggled with the everyday reality of meal preparation. Traditional keto cooking often meant excess oils, messy stovetops, and foods that, while tasty, didn't quite hit the spot when it came to texture.

Enter the air fryer—a device that revolutionized not just my keto cooking, but my entire approach to the ketogenic lifestyle. I still remember the first time I pulled a batch of perfectly crispy, golden-brown keto-breaded chicken tenders from my air fryer. They were everything I'd been missing: crunchy on the outside, juicy on the inside, and achieved with minimal oil and fuss. That moment wasn't just about satisfying a craving; it was an revelation that the keto diet didn't have to mean compromising on texture or taste.

Through years of experimentation, countless recipe tests (and yes, some memorable kitchen fails!), I've discovered that the air fryer is more than just a trendy kitchen gadget—it's an essential tool for anyone serious about keto cooking. This cookbook is the culmination of that journey, designed specifically for those of you who are either starting your keto adventure or looking to enhance it with the magic of air frying.

In these pages, you'll find more than just recipes. You'll discover a comprehensive guide to marrying the principles of ketogenic eating with the convenience and health benefits of air frying. From understanding the science behind why air frying works so well for keto-friendly foods, to mastering the techniques that will elevate your cooking, this book is your roadmap to success.

As a certified nutritionist and long-time keto advocate, I've ensured that every recipe not only adheres to ketogenic principles but also maximizes the potential of your air fryer. Whether you're craving the crunch of breaded fish, the satisfaction of crispy vegetables, or even the joy of keto-friendly desserts, you'll find options that fit your macros and exceed your expectations.

Throughout this book, I'll share not just my successes, but also the lessons learned from my mistakes. You'll benefit from practical tips, troubleshooting advice, and the kind of real-world wisdom that only comes from extensive experience. Together, we'll explore how to make the keto lifestyle not just manageable, but truly enjoyable, one air-fried dish at a time.

Let's begin this flavorful journey together, transforming your keto cooking game with the power of air frying!

GETTING STARTED WITH KETO AIR FRYER

When I unboxed my first air fryer, I'll admit I was both excited and slightly overwhelmed. If you're feeling the same way, don't worry—you're not alone! Think of this chapter as the friendly guidance I wish I'd had when I started my keto air frying adventure.

UNDERSTANDING YOUR AIR FRYER

Let's demystify this ingenious appliance together. At its heart, an air fryer is essentially a compact, high-powered convection oven. It circulates hot air rapidly around your food, creating that coveted crispy exterior that we keto dieters often miss. During my first week of experimenting, I discovered that understanding these key features made all the difference:

- ➤ Temperature Control: Most air fryers range from 175°F to 400°F. I typically start low and adjust up—you can always cook longer, but you can't un-burn food! Through trial and error, I've found that 375°F is my sweet spot for most keto recipes.
- ➤ Timer Function: A blessing for busy cooks! While most air fryers go up to 30 minutes, I've learned to start checking my food at the halfway point. The cooking time can vary significantly between models, so get to know your specific appliance.
- ➤ Basket Capacity: Size matters! I once tried to cook chicken wings for a party all at once—big mistake. For the best results, stick to a single layer of food when possible. If you need to stack, give the basket a good shake every 5 minutes for even cooking.

First Steps with Your Air Fryer

Before you dive into your first recipe, here's my tried-and-true startup routine:

1. Initial Cleaning: Give your air fryer a quick wash with warm, soapy water. I learned this step the hard way when my first batch of keto mozzarella sticks tasted oddly like plastic!
2. Test Run: Run your air fryer empty for 10 minutes at 400°F. This burns off any manufacturing residues and helps you get familiar with the controls. Plus, you'll learn how noisy (or quiet) your model is.
3. Start Simple: Begin with straightforward foods like air-fried vegetables. My first success was simple zucchini chips—just sliced zucchini, olive oil, and salt. The confidence boost from an easy win makes a difference!

Safety First: Lessons from My Kitchen

Over the years, I've developed these safety habits—some through good advice, others through minor mishaps:

1. Always place your air fryer on a heat-resistant surface. That fancy wooden cutting board? Not the best choice, trust me.
2. Keep it at least 4 inches away from walls or other objects. The back of your air fryer expels hot air, and you need proper ventilation.
3. Never use aerosol oil sprays. They can damage the non-stick coating. I use a refillable oil mister instead—it's become my favorite kitchen tool!
4. Invest in good oven mitts. The basket gets HOT, and those thin pot holders won't cut it. Your fingertips will thank you.

KETO AIR FRYER KITCHEN ESSENTIALS

After countless hours in the kitchen and numerous recipe experiments, I've fine-tuned my list of must-have items for successful keto air frying. When I first started, I thought all I needed was the air fryer itself—boy, was I in for a surprise! Let me share the essentials that have made my keto air frying journey so much easier and more enjoyable.

Must-Have Tools

1. Oil Mister: This is my secret weapon! After ruining a basket's non-stick coating with commercial spray oils (a rookie mistake), I invested in a high-quality oil mister. Fill it with your favorite keto-friendly oil for even, controlled coating. I keep two on hand—one for olive oil and another for avocado oil.
2. Kitchen Tongs: Look for silicone-tipped tongs that won't scratch your air fryer basket. I learned this lesson the hard way with metal tongs! The right pair makes it easy to flip foods and remove them safely. Plus, the long handle keeps your hands away from the heat.
3. Meat Thermometer: Trust me, this is non-negotiable. As someone who once served undercooked chicken (never again!), I can't stress enough how important an instant-read thermometer is. It ensures your proteins are perfectly cooked without having to cut into them and lose all those precious juices.
4. Silicone Liners or Parchment Paper: While not necessary for every recipe, these are game-changers for dishes that might stick or when you're using cheese (keto mozzarella sticks, anyone?). Just remember to never use parchment without food on top—it can fly up into the heating element!

The Keto Oil Arsenal

Your choice of oils can make or break your keto air frying experience. Here's what I keep in my kitchen:

- Avocado Oil: My go-to for high-heat cooking. Its high smoke point (500°F) makes it perfect for air frying at higher temperatures. It's also nearly flavorless, letting your seasonings shine through.
- Coconut Oil: Fantastic for adding a subtle sweetness to keto desserts. I've found it works beautifully for air-fried keto donuts!
- Olive Oil: Best for medium-heat cooking and when you want that Mediterranean flavor. I use it mainly for vegetables and chicken.
- Ghee: Clarified butter that adds a rich, buttery flavor without the risk of burning. It's become my secret ingredient for the most amazing keto air-fried vegetables.

Essential Keto Pantry Staples

Over time, I've cultivated a collection of keto-friendly ingredients that have become my air frying staples:

1. Almond Flour: The backbone of many keto breading recipes. I always buy blanched, superfine almond flour for the crispiest results.
2. Coconut Flour: Use sparingly! It's incredibly absorbent. I typically use it in combination with almond flour for the perfect coating texture.
3. Pork Rinds: My absolute favorite for ultra-crispy breading. I keep a food processor dedicated to crushing these into the perfect crumb consistency.
4. Seasonings: Don't underestimate the power of a well-stocked spice rack! My must-haves include:
✓ -Garlic powder
✓ -Onion powder
✓ -Smoked paprika
✓ -Everything bagel seasoning
✓ -Italian herb blend

MASTERING YOUR AIR FRYER

After a year of daily experimentation (and yes, some spectacular failures), I've learned that mastering your air fryer is as much an art as it is a science. Let me share the techniques and tricks that took my keto air frying from merely good to absolutely great.

Essential Techniques

1. Prepping Your Food: The secret to air fryer success starts before you even turn on the machine. I've found that proper prep makes all the difference:
   - Always pat your food dry thoroughly. I can't stress this enough! Moisture is the enemy of crispiness. I keep a stack of paper towels near my prep area just for this.
   - Cut items uniformly for even cooking. Those few extra minutes with your knife pay off in the end. I use a mandoline for vegetables when I need absolute consistency.
   - Season generously—I typically use about 20% more seasoning than I would for regular cooking. Why? Some will blow off during the air frying process. My first few attempts at keto chicken wings were sadly bland until I figured this out!

2. Loading the Basket: Think of your air fryer basket as prime real estate:
   - Arrange food in a single layer when possible. Yes, it might mean cooking in batches, but trust me, it's worth it for the perfect crisp.
   - For layered foods (like my famous keto zucchini chips), shake the basket every 4-5 minutes. I actually set a separate timer on my phone for this.
   - Leave space for air circulation—overcrowding is the fastest way to soggy results. I usually stick to filling the basket only 2/3 full, even if it means cooking an extra batch.

5. Temperature Selection: Through much trial and error, I've developed these temperature guidelines:
   - High heat (380-400°F): Perfect for achieving that crispy exterior on keto-breaded foods. I use this for my pork rind-crusted chicken tenders.
   - Medium heat (350-375°F): The sweet spot for most proteins and vegetables. This range has saved many meals from burning while ensuring thorough cooking.
   - Low heat (300-345°F): Ideal for delicate foods or when reheating leftovers. I discovered this is perfect for keeping keto casseroles warm without drying them out.

6. Timing Guidelines: Timing is everything in air frying, and these are my tried-and-true rules:
   - Always start checking food at the halfway point. I can't tell you how many times this habit has saved a meal!
   - Add 3 minutes to recipes when starting with a cold air fryer. I learned this the hard way with undercooked keto meatballs.
   - Remember that smaller batches cook faster. My rule of thumb: reduce cooking time by 2 minutes for every 25% reduction in food volume.

Keto Air Fryer Stuffed Mushrooms

Prep: 10 mins | Cook: 12 mins | Serves: 4

Ingredients:

- ✓ US: 250g mushrooms (large, stems removed), 100g cream cheese, 50g cheddar cheese (grated), 30g parmesan cheese (grated), 1 tablespoon olive oil, 1 teaspoon garlic powder, 1 teaspoon dried parsley, salt and pepper to taste
- ✓ UK: 250g mushrooms (large, stems removed), 100g cream cheese, 50g cheddar cheese (grated), 30g parmesan cheese (grated), 1 tablespoon olive oil, 1 teaspoon garlic powder, 1 teaspoon dried parsley, salt and pepper to taste

Instructions:

1. Preheat your air fryer to 200°C (390°F).
2. In a bowl, mix the cream cheese, cheddar, parmesan, garlic powder, parsley, salt, and pepper until well combined.
3. Lightly brush the mushroom caps with olive oil, then stuff each mushroom with the cheese mixture.
4. Place the stuffed mushrooms in the air fryer basket in a single layer.
5. Air fry for 10-12 minutes until the mushrooms are tender and the tops are golden and bubbly.
6. Serve hot as a perfect keto-friendly starter or side!

Nutritional info: Calories: 140 | Fat: 12g | Carbs: 3g | Protein: 5g

Air Fryer Function: Use the air fry setting for quick, even cooking that gives a crispy texture without excess oil.

Keto Air Fryer Cauliflower Rice (4 Ways)

Prep: 5 mins | Cook: 8 mins | Serves: 4

Ingredients:

- ✓ US: 400g cauliflower (riced), 1 tablespoon olive oil, salt, pepper, and seasonings of choice (e.g., turmeric for golden rice, soy sauce for Asian style)
- ✓ UK: 400g cauliflower (riced), 1 tablespoon olive oil, salt, pepper, and seasonings of choice (e.g., turmeric for golden rice, soy sauce for Asian style)

Instructions:

1. Preheat your air fryer to 180°C (350°F).
2. Toss the riced cauliflower with olive oil, salt, pepper, and any preferred seasonings.
3. Spread the cauliflower rice in the air fryer basket, ensuring it's evenly distributed.
4. Air fry for 7-8 minutes, shaking halfway through to ensure even cooking.
5. Once golden and slightly crispy, remove from the air fryer and serve.

Nutritional info: Calories: 55 | Fat: 4g | Carbs: 3g | Protein: 2g

Air Fryer Function: The air fry function crisps the cauliflower without turning it mushy, providing a satisfying texture.

Keto Air Fryer Stuffed Peppers

Prep: 15 mins | Cook: 15 mins | Serves: 4

Ingredients:

- ✓ US: 4 medium bell peppers (halved and seeded), 200g minced beef, 100g mozzarella cheese, 1 small onion (diced), 1 tablespoon olive oil, 1 teaspoon cumin, 1 teaspoon paprika, salt, pepper
- ✓ UK: 4 medium bell peppers (halved and seeded), 200g minced beef, 100g mozzarella cheese, 1 small onion (diced), 1 tablespoon olive oil, 1 teaspoon cumin, 1 teaspoon paprika, salt, pepper

Instructions:

1. Preheat your air fryer to 190°C (375°F).
2. Heat the olive oil in a pan, sauté the onion until soft, then add minced beef, cumin, paprika, salt, and pepper. Cook until browned.
3. Stuff the bell peppers with the beef mixture and top with mozzarella.
4. Place the peppers in the air fryer and cook for 12-15 minutes, until the peppers are tender and the cheese is melted and golden.
5. Serve warm, garnished with fresh herbs if desired.

Nutritional info: Calories: 210 | Fat: 14g | Carbs: 6g | Protein: 18g

Air Fryer Function: The air fry setting ensures even cooking of the peppers while keeping the filling moist and cheesy.

Keto Air Fryer Loaded Mashed Cauliflower

Prep: 10 mins | Cook: 12 mins | Serves: 4

Ingredients:

- ✓ US: 500g cauliflower florets, 50g cream cheese, 50g cheddar cheese (grated), 2 slices bacon (cooked and crumbled), 2 tablespoons butter, salt, pepper, chives (for garnish)
- ✓ UK: 500g cauliflower florets, 50g cream cheese, 50g cheddar cheese (grated), 2 slices bacon (cooked and crumbled), 2 tablespoons butter, salt, pepper, chives (for garnish)

Instructions:

1. Preheat your air fryer to 200°C (390°F).
2. Steam or boil the cauliflower until soft, then drain thoroughly.
3. In a bowl, mash the cauliflower with cream cheese, butter, salt, and pepper until smooth.
4. Transfer the mashed cauliflower to an air fryer-safe dish. Top with cheddar cheese and bacon crumbles.
5. Air fry for 10-12 minutes until the top is golden and crispy.
6. Garnish with chopped chives and serve.

Nutritional info: Calories: 230 | Fat: 18g | Carbs: 5g | Protein: 8g

Air Fryer Function: The air fry function crisps the topping while keeping the mashed cauliflower creamy.

Keto Air Fryer Coleslaw

Prep: 10 mins | Cook: 0 mins | Serves: 4

Ingredients:

- ✓ US: 200g cabbage (shredded), 1 small carrot (grated), 2 tablespoons mayonnaise, 1 tablespoon apple cider vinegar, 1 teaspoon Dijon mustard, salt, pepper
- ✓ UK: 200g cabbage (shredded), 1 small carrot (grated), 2 tablespoons mayonnaise, 1 tablespoon apple cider vinegar, 1 teaspoon Dijon mustard, salt, pepper

Instructions:

1. In a large bowl, mix the cabbage and grated carrot.
2. In a small bowl, whisk together mayonnaise, vinegar, mustard, salt, and pepper.
3. Pour the dressing over the vegetables and toss until well combined.
4. Chill for at least 30 minutes before serving to allow the flavours to meld.

Nutritional info: Calories: 85 | Fat: 7g | Carbs: 5g | Protein: 1g

Air Fryer Function: While this recipe doesn't use cooking, serve it alongside your air-fried dishes for a refreshing contrast!

Keto Air Fryer Ratatouille

Prep: 10 mins | Cook: 20 mins | Serves: 4

Ingredients:

- ✓ US: 1 small aubergine (chopped), 1 courgette (chopped), 1 red pepper (chopped), 1 onion (chopped), 2 cloves garlic (minced), 2 tablespoons olive oil, 1 teaspoon dried thyme, salt, pepper
- ✓ UK: 1 small aubergine (chopped), 1 courgette (chopped), 1 red pepper (chopped), 1 onion (chopped), 2 cloves garlic (minced), 2 tablespoons olive oil, 1 teaspoon dried thyme, salt, pepper

Instructions:

1. Preheat your air fryer to 180°C (350°F).
2. Toss the aubergine, courgette, red pepper, and onion with olive oil, garlic, thyme, salt, and pepper.
3. Spread the vegetables evenly in the air fryer basket.
4. Air fry for 18-20 minutes, shaking the basket halfway through, until the vegetables are soft and slightly charred.
5. Serve hot as a side or mix with grilled meats for a full meal.

Nutritional info: Calories: 120 | Fat: 9g | Carbs: 8g | Protein: 2g

Air Fryer Function: The air fry setting allows the vegetables to caramelise beautifully without drying out.

Keto Air Fryer Spaghetti Squash

Prep: 10 mins | Cook: 25 mins | Serves: 4

Ingredients:

- ✓ US: 1 medium spaghetti squash (about 1kg), 2 tablespoons olive oil, 1 teaspoon garlic powder, salt, pepper, 50g grated parmesan cheese (optional)
- ✓ UK: 1 medium spaghetti squash (about 1kg), 2 tablespoons olive oil, 1 teaspoon garlic powder, salt, pepper, 50g grated parmesan cheese (optional)

Instructions:

1. Preheat your air fryer to 190°C (375°F).
2. Cut the spaghetti squash in half lengthwise and scoop out the seeds.
3. Drizzle olive oil over the squash, then season with garlic powder, salt, and pepper.
4. Place the squash halves, cut side up, in the air fryer basket.
5. Air fry for 20-25 minutes, until the flesh is tender and easily shredded with a fork.
6. Use a fork to scrape out the spaghetti-like strands and top with grated parmesan if desired.

Nutritional info: Calories: 90 | Fat: 6g | Carbs: 7g | Protein: 2g

Air Fryer Function: The air fry setting gives the squash a tender texture with slightly crispy edges, perfect for a low-carb pasta alternative.

Keto Air Fryer Cheesy Cauliflower Tots

Prep: 15 mins | Cook: 12 mins | Serves: 4

Ingredients:

- ✓ US: 400g cauliflower florets, 1 large egg, 50g cheddar cheese (grated), 30g almond flour, 1 teaspoon garlic powder, salt, pepper
- ✓ UK: 400g cauliflower florets, 1 large egg, 50g cheddar cheese (grated), 30g almond flour, 1 teaspoon garlic powder, salt, pepper

Instructions:

1. Preheat your air fryer to 200°C (390°F).
2. Steam or boil the cauliflower florets until tender, then drain and mash them well.
3. In a bowl, combine the mashed cauliflower with the egg, cheddar cheese, almond flour, garlic powder, salt, and pepper.
4. Shape the mixture into small, tot-shaped bites and place them in the air fryer basket.
5. Air fry for 10-12 minutes, flipping halfway through, until golden and crispy.
6. Serve with your favourite keto-friendly dipping sauce.

Nutritional info: Calories: 110 | Fat: 8g | Carbs: 4g | Protein: 5g

Air Fryer Function: The air fry function crisps the tots perfectly, offering a crunchy exterior while keeping the inside soft.

Keto Air Fryer Creamed Spinach

Prep: 5 mins | Cook: 10 mins | Serves: 4

Ingredients:

- ✓ US: 200g fresh spinach, 50g cream cheese, 30ml heavy cream, 1 tablespoon butter, 1 clove garlic (minced), 20g parmesan cheese (grated), salt, pepper
- ✓ UK: 200g fresh spinach, 50g cream cheese, 30ml double cream, 1 tablespoon butter, 1 clove garlic (minced), 20g parmesan cheese (grated), salt, pepper

Instructions:

1. Preheat your air fryer to 180°C (350°F).
2. In a pan, melt the butter and sauté the garlic until fragrant.
3. Add the spinach and cook until wilted. Remove from heat and stir in the cream cheese, heavy cream, parmesan, salt, and pepper.
4. Transfer the mixture to an air fryer-safe dish.
5. Air fry for 8-10 minutes until bubbling and golden on top.
6. Serve warm as a creamy, indulgent side.

Nutritional info: Calories: 170 | Fat: 14g | Carbs: 3g | Protein: 5g

Air Fryer Function: The air fryer creates a beautiful golden crust on top of the creamy spinach.

Keto Air Fryer Mediterranean Veggies

Prep: 10 mins | Cook: 15 mins | Serves: 4

Ingredients:

- ✓ US: 1 small aubergine (chopped), 1 courgette (chopped), 1 red onion (chopped), 1 yellow bell pepper (chopped), 2 tablespoons olive oil, 1 teaspoon dried oregano, 1 teaspoon garlic powder, salt, pepper
- ✓ UK: 1 small aubergine (chopped), 1 courgette (chopped), 1 red onion (chopped), 1 yellow bell pepper (chopped), 2 tablespoons olive oil, 1 teaspoon dried oregano, 1 teaspoon garlic powder, salt, pepper

Instructions:

1. Preheat your air fryer to 190°C (375°F).
2. In a bowl, toss the chopped vegetables with olive oil, oregano, garlic powder, salt, and pepper.
3. Spread the vegetables evenly in the air fryer basket.
4. Air fry for 12-15 minutes, shaking halfway through, until the veggies are tender and slightly charred.
5. Serve warm with a drizzle of olive oil or lemon juice.

Nutritional info: Calories: 120 | Fat: 9g | Carbs: 8g | Protein: 2g

Air Fryer Function: The air fry setting ensures the vegetables are evenly roasted and caramelised without the need for much oil.

Keto Air Fryer Cinnamon Sugar Nuts

Prep: 5 mins | Cook: 10 mins | Serves: 4

Ingredients:

- ✓ US: 200g mixed nuts, 2 tablespoons erythritol, 1 teaspoon ground cinnamon, 1 tablespoon melted butter
- ✓ UK: 200g mixed nuts, 2 tablespoons erythritol, 1 teaspoon ground cinnamon, 1 tablespoon melted butter

Instructions:

1. Preheat your air fryer to 160°C (320°F).
2. In a bowl, toss the mixed nuts with melted butter, erythritol, and cinnamon until evenly coated.
3. Spread the nuts in a single layer in the air fryer basket.
4. Air fry for 8-10 minutes, shaking the basket halfway through, until golden and fragrant.
5. Let cool before serving, and enjoy a crunchy, sweet snack.

Nutritional info: Calories: 210 | Fat: 18g | Carbs: 4g | Protein: 6g

Air Fryer Function: Use the air fry setting to toast the nuts evenly while keeping them crunchy.

Keto Air Fryer Coconut Macaroons (3 Ways)

Prep: 10 mins | Cook: 12 mins | Serves: 12 macaroons

Ingredients:

- ✓ US: 200g shredded coconut (unsweetened), 2 large egg whites, 50g erythritol, 1 teaspoon vanilla extract
- ✓ UK: 200g shredded coconut (unsweetened), 2 large egg whites, 50g erythritol, 1 teaspoon vanilla extract

For flavour variations:

- ✓ Chocolate Drizzle: 50g sugar-free dark chocolate, melted
- ✓ Lemon Zest: 1 tablespoon lemon zest
- ✓ Almond Joy: 50g chopped almonds, 2 tablespoons sugar-free chocolate chips

Instructions:

1. Preheat your air fryer to 170°C (340°F).
2. In a bowl, whisk the egg whites until frothy, then fold in the shredded coconut, erythritol, and vanilla.
3. Shape the mixture into small balls and place them in the air fryer basket.
4. Air fry for 10-12 minutes until golden brown.
5. Add your chosen flavour variations after cooling: drizzle with melted chocolate, sprinkle with lemon zest, or top with chopped almonds and chocolate chips.

Nutritional info (per macaroon): Calories: 90 | Fat: 7g | Carbs: 3g | Protein: 1g

Air Fryer Function: The air fry setting gives these macaroons a crisp exterior with a soft, chewy centre.

Keto Air Fryer Chocolate Chip Cookies (3 Ways)

Prep: 10 mins | Cook: 8 mins | Serves: 12 cookies

Ingredients:

- ✓ US: 100g almond flour, 50g coconut flour, 50g butter (melted), 50g sugar-free chocolate chips, 2 tablespoons erythritol, 1 large egg, 1 teaspoon vanilla extract, ½ teaspoon baking powder
- ✓ UK: 100g almond flour, 50g coconut flour, 50g butter (melted), 50g sugar-free chocolate chips, 2 tablespoons erythritol, 1 large egg, 1 teaspoon vanilla extract, ½ teaspoon baking powder

For variations:

- ✓ Double Chocolate: Add 1 tablespoon cocoa powder
- ✓ Peanut Butter: Swap 2 tablespoons of butter for peanut butter
- ✓ Coconut Flake: Add 2 tablespoons shredded coconut

Instructions:

1. Preheat your air fryer to 180°C (350°F).
2. In a bowl, mix the almond flour, coconut flour, erythritol, and baking powder.
3. Add the melted butter, egg, and vanilla extract, and stir until a dough forms. Fold in the chocolate chips.
4. Shape the dough into small balls, flatten slightly, and place them in the air fryer basket.
5. Air fry for 6-8 minutes until golden brown around the edges.

Nutritional info (per cookie): Calories: 95 | Fat: 8g | Carbs: 3g | Protein: 2g

Air Fryer Function: Use the air fry setting for perfectly crispy cookies with a soft centre.

Keto Air Fryer Brownies (2 Ways)

Prep: 10 mins | Cook: 12 mins | Serves: 8

Ingredients:

- ✓ US: 100g almond flour, 50g cocoa powder, 50g butter (melted), 50g erythritol, 2 large eggs, 1 teaspoon vanilla extract, ½ teaspoon baking powder
- ✓ UK: 100g almond flour, 50g cocoa powder, 50g butter (melted), 50g erythritol, 2 large eggs, 1 teaspoon vanilla extract, ½ teaspoon baking powder

For variations:

- ✓ Nutty Brownies: Add 50g chopped walnuts
- ✓ Choc Chip Brownies: Fold in 50g sugar-free chocolate chips

Instructions:

1. Preheat your air fryer to 170°C (340°F).
2. In a bowl, mix the almond flour, cocoa powder, erythritol, and baking powder.
3. Add the melted butter, eggs, and vanilla extract, and stir until well combined.
4. Pour the batter into an air fryer-safe dish.
5. Air fry for 10-12 minutes until the brownies are set but still slightly gooey in the centre.

Nutritional info (per brownie): Calories: 120 | Fat: 10g | Carbs: 4g | Protein: 3g

Air Fryer Function: The air fry setting bakes the brownies with a crispy top and fudgy centre.

Keto Air Fryer Apple Crisps

Prep: 5 mins | Cook: 15 mins | Serves: 4

Ingredients:

- ✓ US: 2 medium Granny Smith apples (thinly sliced), 1 tablespoon cinnamon, 2 tablespoons erythritol
- ✓ UK: 2 medium Granny Smith apples (thinly sliced), 1 tablespoon cinnamon, 2 tablespoons erythritol

Instructions:

1. Preheat your air fryer to 160°C (320°F).
2. In a bowl, toss the apple slices with cinnamon and erythritol.
3. Lay the apple slices in a single layer in the air fryer basket.
4. Air fry for 12-15 minutes, flipping halfway through, until crisp.
5. Let cool before serving for a crunchy, sweet snack.

Nutritional info: Calories: 60 | Fat: 0g | Carbs: 12g | Protein: 0g

Air Fryer Function: The air fry setting creates perfectly crispy apple slices with minimal oil.

Keto Air Fryer Pumpkin Custard

Prep: 10 mins | Cook: 15 mins | Serves: 4

Ingredients:

- ✓ US: 200g pumpkin puree, 100ml heavy cream, 2 large eggs, 50g erythritol, 1 teaspoon pumpkin spice, 1 teaspoon vanilla extract
- ✓ UK: 200g pumpkin puree, 100ml double cream, 2 large eggs, 50g erythritol, 1 teaspoon pumpkin spice, 1 teaspoon vanilla extract

Instructions:

1. Preheat your air fryer to 160°C (320°F).
2. In a bowl, whisk together the pumpkin puree, cream, eggs, erythritol, pumpkin spice, and vanilla extract.
3. Pour the mixture into air fryer-safe ramekins.
4. Air fry for 12-15 minutes until the custard is set but still slightly wobbly in the centre.
5. Let cool before serving for a creamy, spiced dessert.

Nutritional info: Calories: 160 | Fat: 12g | Carbs: 6g | Protein: 4g

Air Fryer Function: The air fry setting gently cooks the custard for a smooth, creamy texture.

Keto Air Fryer Lemon Curd Tarts

Prep: 15 mins | Cook: 10 mins | Serves: 6

Ingredients:

- ✓ US: 100g almond flour, 50g butter (melted), 2 tablespoons erythritol, 3 large egg yolks, 50ml lemon juice, 50g erythritol (for curd), 1 teaspoon lemon zest
- ✓ UK: 100g almond flour, 50g butter (melted), 2 tablespoons erythritol, 3 large egg yolks, 50ml lemon juice, 50g erythritol (for curd), 1 teaspoon lemon zest

Instructions:

1. Preheat your air fryer to 170°C (340°F).
2. Mix the almond flour, melted butter, and 2 tablespoons erythritol to form the tart crust. Press into tart cases.
3. Air fry the crusts for 5-7 minutes until golden.
4. Meanwhile, whisk the egg yolks, lemon juice, 50g erythritol, and lemon zest in a saucepan over low heat until thickened.
5. Spoon the lemon curd into the cooled tart cases and chill before serving.

Nutritional info (per tart): Calories: 140 | Fat: 12g | Carbs: 4g | Protein: 3g

Air Fryer Function: Use the air fry setting to crisp up the almond flour tart shells.

Keto Air Fryer Berry Cobbler

Prep: 10 mins | Cook: 12 mins | Serves: 4

Ingredients:

- ✓ US: 200g mixed berries, 50g almond flour, 1 tablespoon coconut flour, 50g butter (cold), 2 tablespoons erythritol, 1 teaspoon vanilla extract
- ✓ UK: 200g mixed berries, 50g almond flour, 1 tablespoon coconut flour, 50g butter (cold), 2 tablespoons erythritol, 1 teaspoon vanilla extract

Instructions:

1. Preheat your air fryer to 180°C (350°F).
2. Place the mixed berries in an air fryer-safe dish.
3. In a bowl, mix the almond flour, coconut flour, erythritol, and vanilla. Rub in the cold butter to form a crumbly topping.
4. Sprinkle the topping over the berries.
5. Air fry for 10-12 minutes until the topping is golden and crisp.

Nutritional info (per serving): Calories: 150 | Fat: 12g | Carbs: 7g | Protein: 2g

Air Fryer Function: The air fry setting gives the cobbler a crisp topping while keeping the berries juicy.

Keto Air Fryer Chocolate Lava Cakes

Prep: 10 mins | Cook: 8 mins | Serves: 4

Ingredients:

- ✓ US: 100g sugar-free dark chocolate, 50g butter (melted), 2 large eggs, 50g erythritol, 50g almond flour, 1 teaspoon vanilla extract
- ✓ UK: 100g sugar-free dark chocolate, 50g butter (melted), 2 large eggs, 50g erythritol, 50g almond flour, 1 teaspoon vanilla extract

Instructions:

1. Preheat your air fryer to 190°C (375°F).
2. Melt the chocolate and butter together in the microwave, then stir in the eggs, erythritol, almond flour, and vanilla extract.
3. Pour the mixture into air fryer-safe ramekins.
4. Air fry for 6-8 minutes until the edges are set but the centre is still gooey.
5. Serve immediately for a rich, molten chocolate treat.

Nutritional info (per cake): Calories: 180 | Fat: 14g | Carbs: 6g | Protein: 4g

Air Fryer Function: Use the air fry setting for the perfect molten centre.

Keto Air Fryer Peanut Butter Cups

Prep: 10 mins | Cook: 5 mins | Serves: 6

Ingredients:

- ✓ US: 100g sugar-free dark chocolate, 50g smooth peanut butter, 2 tablespoons coconut oil, 1 tablespoon erythritol
- ✓ UK: 100g sugar-free dark chocolate, 50g smooth peanut butter, 2 tablespoons coconut oil, 1 tablespoon erythritol

Instructions:

1. Preheat your air fryer to 160°C (320°F).
2. Melt the chocolate and coconut oil together in the microwave.
3. Pour half the chocolate mixture into silicone cupcake moulds.
4. Add a teaspoon of peanut butter into the centre of each mould, then top with the remaining chocolate.
5. Air fry for 3-5 minutes until set.

Nutritional info (per cup): Calories: 120 | Fat: 10g | Carbs: 5g | Protein: 3g

Air Fryer Function: The air fry setting helps the chocolate set quickly for perfectly shaped cups.

Keto Air Fryer Marinara Sauce

Prep: 5 mins | Cook: 20 mins | Serves: 6

Ingredients:

- ✓ US: 400g canned tomatoes, 2 tablespoons olive oil, 2 garlic cloves (minced), 1 teaspoon oregano, 1 teaspoon basil, salt and pepper to taste
- ✓ UK: 400g canned tomatoes, 2 tablespoons olive oil, 2 garlic cloves (minced), 1 teaspoon oregano, 1 teaspoon basil, salt and pepper to taste

Instructions:

1. Preheat your air fryer to 180°C (350°F).
2. In an air fryer-safe dish, mix the tomatoes, olive oil, garlic, oregano, basil, salt, and pepper.
3. Air fry for 15-20 minutes, stirring halfway through.
4. Once cooked, blend the sauce until smooth or leave it chunky for a rustic feel.

Nutritional info (per serving): Calories: 80 | Fat: 6g | Carbs: 5g | Protein: 1g

Air Fryer Function: Use the air fry setting for even cooking and sauce reduction.

Keto Air Fryer Hollandaise Sauce

Prep: 5 mins | Cook: 8 mins | Serves: 4

Ingredients:

- ✓ US: 3 egg yolks, 100g butter (melted), 1 tablespoon lemon juice, pinch of cayenne, salt to taste
- ✓ UK: 3 egg yolks, 100g butter (melted), 1 tablespoon lemon juice, pinch of cayenne, salt to taste

Instructions:

1. Preheat your air fryer to 75°C (165°F).
2. In a blender, combine egg yolks, lemon juice, cayenne, and salt.
3. Slowly drizzle in the melted butter while blending until the sauce thickens.
4. Pour into an air fryer-safe ramekin and keep warm in the air fryer for 5-8 minutes.

Nutritional info (per serving): Calories: 200 | Fat: 22g | Carbs: 1g | Protein: 2g

Air Fryer Function: Use the warm setting to keep the hollandaise at the perfect consistency.

Keto Air Fryer Barbecue Sauce

Prep: 5 mins | Cook: 10 mins | Serves: 8

Ingredients:

- ✓ US: 200g tomato paste, 2 tablespoons apple cider vinegar, 2 tablespoons Worcestershire sauce, 1 tablespoon smoked paprika, 1 teaspoon garlic powder, 1 teaspoon onion powder, 2 tablespoons erythritol, salt and pepper to taste
- ✓ UK: 200g tomato paste, 2 tablespoons apple cider vinegar, 2 tablespoons Worcestershire sauce, 1 tablespoon smoked paprika, 1 teaspoon garlic powder, 1 teaspoon onion powder, 2 tablespoons erythritol, salt and pepper to taste

Instructions:

1. Preheat your air fryer to 180°C (350°F).
2. Combine all ingredients in an air fryer-safe dish.
3. Air fry for 8-10 minutes, stirring halfway, until the sauce thickens.

Nutritional info (per serving): Calories: 35 | Fat: 0g | Carbs: 4g | Protein: 1g

Air Fryer Function: The air fry setting helps the sauce reduce and intensify in flavour.

Keto Buffalo Sauce

Prep: 5 mins | Cook: 5 mins | Serves: 4

Ingredients:

- ✓ US: 100g butter, 100ml hot sauce (Frank's RedHot), 1 tablespoon apple cider vinegar, 1 teaspoon garlic powder
- ✓ UK: 100g butter, 100ml hot sauce (Frank's RedHot), 1 tablespoon apple cider vinegar, 1 teaspoon garlic powder

Instructions:

1. Preheat your air fryer to 160°C (320°F).
2. In an air fryer-safe bowl, melt the butter for 2 minutes.
3. Stir in the hot sauce, vinegar, and garlic powder until well combined.
4. Air fry for another 3 minutes to allow the flavours to meld.

Nutritional info (per serving): Calories: 120 | Fat: 12g | Carbs: 1g | Protein: 1g

Air Fryer Function: Use the warm setting to perfectly melt the butter.

Keto Air Fryer Ranch Dressing

Prep: 5 mins | Cook: 0 mins | Serves: 6

Ingredients:

- ✓ US: 120g sour cream, 60g mayonnaise, 1 tablespoon apple cider vinegar, 1 teaspoon garlic powder, 1 teaspoon onion powder, 1 tablespoon fresh dill (chopped), salt and pepper to taste
- ✓ UK: 120g sour cream, 60g mayonnaise, 1 tablespoon apple cider vinegar, 1 teaspoon garlic powder, 1 teaspoon onion powder, 1 tablespoon fresh dill (chopped), salt and pepper to taste

Instructions:

1. Combine all the ingredients in a bowl and whisk until smooth.
2. Chill in the fridge for at least 30 minutes before serving.

Nutritional info (per serving): Calories: 100 | Fat: 10g | Carbs: 1g | Protein: 1g

Air Fryer Function: None, but this pairs beautifully with air-fried keto snacks.

Keto Air Fryer Blue Cheese Dressing

Prep: 5 mins | Cook: 0 mins | Serves: 6

Ingredients:

- ✓ US: 100g blue cheese (crumbled), 120g sour cream, 60g mayonnaise, 1 tablespoon lemon juice, 1 tablespoon apple cider vinegar, salt and pepper to taste
- ✓ UK: 100g blue cheese (crumbled), 120g sour cream, 60g mayonnaise, 1 tablespoon lemon juice, 1 tablespoon apple cider vinegar, salt and pepper to taste

Instructions:

1. In a bowl, whisk together the sour cream, mayonnaise, lemon juice, and vinegar.
2. Fold in the crumbled blue cheese.
3. Season with salt and pepper to taste.

Nutritional info (per serving): Calories: 110 | Fat: 11g | Carbs: 1g | Protein: 2g

Air Fryer Function: None, but perfect for air-fried wings or veggies.

Keto Air Fryer Spinach Artichoke Dip

Prep: 10 mins | Cook: 10 mins | Serves: 4

Ingredients:
- ✓ US: 100g spinach (fresh or frozen), 100g artichoke hearts (chopped), 100g cream cheese, 50g sour cream, 50g mozzarella (grated), 1 teaspoon garlic powder, salt and pepper to taste
- ✓ UK: 100g spinach (fresh or frozen), 100g artichoke hearts (chopped), 100g cream cheese, 50g sour cream, 50g mozzarella (grated), 1 teaspoon garlic powder, salt and pepper to taste

Instructions:
1. Preheat your air fryer to 180°C (350°F).
2. In an air fryer-safe dish, combine all the ingredients.
3. Air fry for 8-10 minutes, stirring halfway, until the dip is hot and bubbly.

Nutritional info (per serving): Calories: 190 | Fat: 17g | Carbs: 3g | Protein: 5g

Air Fryer Function: The air fry setting ensures a hot, gooey dip with a slightly crisp top.

Keto Air Fryer Bacon Jam

Prep: 10 mins | Cook: 15 mins | Serves: 8

Ingredients:
- ✓ US: 200g bacon (chopped), 1 small onion (chopped), 1 tablespoon balsamic vinegar, 2 tablespoons erythritol, 1 teaspoon smoked paprika, 100ml water
- ✓ UK: 200g bacon (chopped), 1 small onion (chopped), 1 tablespoon balsamic vinegar, 2 tablespoons erythritol, 1 teaspoon smoked paprika, 100ml water

Instructions:
1. Preheat your air fryer to 180°C (350°F).
2. Fry the bacon in an air fryer-safe pan for 8-10 minutes, stirring occasionally.
3. Add the onion, balsamic vinegar, erythritol, paprika, and water. Air fry for another 5 minutes until reduced to a jam-like consistency.

Nutritional info (per serving): Calories: 90 | Fat: 7g | Carbs: 2g | Protein: 5g

Air Fryer Function: The air fry setting crisps the bacon while keeping the jam soft and sweet.

Keto Air Fryer Onion Dip

Prep: 5 mins | Cook: 12 mins | Serves: 6

Ingredients:

- ✓ US: 2 onions (sliced), 120g sour cream, 60g mayonnaise, 1 teaspoon garlic powder, salt and pepper to taste
- ✓ UK: 2 onions (sliced), 120g sour cream, 60g mayonnaise, 1 teaspoon garlic powder, salt and pepper to taste

Instructions:

1. Preheat your air fryer to 180°C (350°F).
2. Air fry the sliced onions in an air fryer-safe pan for 10-12 minutes until caramelised.
3. Once cooled, mix the onions with sour cream, mayonnaise, and garlic powder.
4. Season with salt and pepper.

Nutritional info (per serving): Calories: 100 | Fat: 9g | Carbs: 3g | Protein: 1g

Air Fryer Function: Use the air fry setting to perfectly caramelise the onions.

Keto Air Fryer Curry Dressing

Prep: 5 mins | Cook: 0 mins | Serves: 4

Ingredients:

- ✓ US: 120g mayonnaise, 1 teaspoon curry powder, 1 tablespoon apple cider vinegar, 1 teaspoon garlic powder, salt to taste
- ✓ UK: 120g mayonnaise, 1 teaspoon curry powder, 1 tablespoon apple cider vinegar, 1 teaspoon garlic powder, salt to taste

Instructions:

1. Combine all the ingredients in a bowl and whisk until smooth.
2. Chill for at least 30 minutes before serving.

Nutritional info (per serving): Calories: 110 | Fat: 12g | Carbs: 1g | Protein: 0g

Air Fryer Function: None, but perfect for drizzling over air-fried chicken or vegetables.

Keto Air Fryer Fajitas

Prep: 10 mins | Cook: 12 mins | Serves: 4

Ingredients:

- ✓ US: 500g beef sirloin (sliced), 1 red pepper (sliced), 1 green pepper (sliced), 1 onion (sliced), 2 tablespoons olive oil, 1 teaspoon cumin, 1 teaspoon paprika, 1 teaspoon garlic powder, 1 tablespoon lime juice, salt, and pepper to taste
- ✓ UK: 500g beef sirloin (sliced), 1 red pepper (sliced), 1 green pepper (sliced), 1 onion (sliced), 2 tablespoons olive oil, 1 teaspoon cumin, 1 teaspoon paprika, 1 teaspoon garlic powder, 1 tablespoon lime juice, salt, and pepper to taste

Instructions:

1. Preheat your air fryer to 200°C (390°F).
2. In a bowl, toss the beef, peppers, and onion with olive oil, cumin, paprika, garlic powder, lime juice, salt, and pepper.
3. Spread the mixture in an even layer in the air fryer basket.
4. Air fry for 10-12 minutes, shaking halfway through, until the beef is cooked and the veggies are tender.
5. Serve with keto-friendly tortillas or over lettuce for a low-carb fajita bowl.

Nutritional info (per serving): Calories: 320 | Fat: 22g | Carbs: 5g | Protein: 25g

Air Fryer Function: Air fry setting for a crispy, charred texture on the beef and veggies.

Keto Air Fryer Steak Bites

Prep: 5 mins | Cook: 8 mins | Serves: 4

Ingredients:

- ✓ US: 500g ribeye steak (cut into 1-inch cubes), 2 tablespoons olive oil, 1 teaspoon garlic powder, 1 teaspoon onion powder, salt, and pepper to taste
- ✓ UK: 500g ribeye steak (cut into 1-inch cubes), 2 tablespoons olive oil, 1 teaspoon garlic powder, 1 teaspoon onion powder, salt, and pepper to taste

Instructions:

1. Preheat your air fryer to 200°C (390°F).
2. Toss the steak cubes with olive oil, garlic powder, onion powder, salt, and pepper.
3. Place the steak bites in the air fryer basket in a single layer.
4. Air fry for 6-8 minutes, shaking halfway, until the steak bites are golden brown and cooked to your liking.
5. Serve with a side of garlic butter for dipping.

Nutritional info (per serving): Calories: 350 | Fat: 28g | Carbs: 1g | Protein: 23g

Air Fryer Function: Air fry setting to sear and brown the steak bites quickly.

Keto Air Fryer Pot Roast

Prep: 10 mins | Cook: 1 hour 30 mins | Serves: 6

Ingredients:

- ✓ US: 1.2kg beef chuck roast, 2 tablespoons olive oil, 1 onion (sliced), 2 garlic cloves (minced), 1 teaspoon thyme, 1 teaspoon rosemary, 100ml beef broth, salt, and pepper to taste
- ✓ UK: 1.2kg beef chuck roast, 2 tablespoons olive oil, 1 onion (sliced), 2 garlic cloves (minced), 1 teaspoon thyme, 1 teaspoon rosemary, 100ml beef broth, salt, and pepper to taste

Instructions:

1. Preheat your air fryer to 160°C (320°F).
2. Rub the chuck roast with olive oil, thyme, rosemary, salt, and pepper.
3. Place the roast in the air fryer basket and cook for 1 hour, turning halfway through.
4. Add the onion, garlic, and beef broth to the air fryer, then cook for another 30 minutes, or until the roast is tender and juicy.
5. Let the roast rest for 10 minutes before slicing and serving.

Nutritional info (per serving): Calories: 450 | Fat: 35g | Carbs: 2g | Protein: 35g

Air Fryer Function: Roast setting for a slow, even cook and tender meat.

Keto Air Fryer Flat Iron Steak

Prep: 5 mins | Cook: 10 mins | Serves: 2

Ingredients:

- ✓ US: 400g flat iron steak, 1 tablespoon olive oil, 1 teaspoon garlic powder, salt, and pepper to taste
- ✓ UK: 400g flat iron steak, 1 tablespoon olive oil, 1 teaspoon garlic powder, salt, and pepper to taste

Instructions:

1. Preheat your air fryer to 200°C (390°F).
2. Rub the flat iron steak with olive oil, garlic powder, salt, and pepper.
3. Place the steak in the air fryer basket.
4. Air fry for 8-10 minutes, flipping halfway through, until the steak reaches your desired doneness.
5. Let the steak rest for 5 minutes before slicing.

Nutritional info (per serving): Calories: 300 | Fat: 22g | Carbs: 0g | Protein: 25g

Air Fryer Function: Air fry setting to achieve a quick sear on the outside while keeping the inside tender.

Keto Air Fryer Prime Rib

Prep: 10 mins | Cook: 1 hour | Serves: 4

Ingredients:

- ✓ US: 1.5kg prime rib, 2 tablespoons olive oil, 1 tablespoon rosemary, 1 tablespoon thyme, 2 garlic cloves (minced), salt, and pepper to taste
- ✓ UK: 1.5kg prime rib, 2 tablespoons olive oil, 1 tablespoon rosemary, 1 tablespoon thyme, 2 garlic cloves (minced), salt, and pepper to taste

Instructions:

1. Preheat your air fryer to 180°C (350°F).
2. Rub the prime rib with olive oil, rosemary, thyme, garlic, salt, and pepper.
3. Place the prime rib in the air fryer basket.
4. Air fry for 50-60 minutes, depending on your desired level of doneness, turning halfway through.
5. Let the prime rib rest for 15 minutes before carving.

Nutritional info (per serving): Calories: 600 | Fat: 50g | Carbs: 1g | Protein: 35g

Air Fryer Function: Roast setting for slow, even cooking and a crispy crust.

Keto Air Fryer Rouladen

Prep: 15 mins | Cook: 25 mins | Serves: 4

Ingredients:

- ✓ US: 4 beef rouladen (thin beef slices), 100g bacon (chopped), 1 onion (chopped), 2 pickles (sliced), 1 tablespoon mustard, 2 tablespoons olive oil, salt, and pepper to taste
- ✓ UK: 4 beef rouladen (thin beef slices), 100g bacon (chopped), 1 onion (chopped), 2 pickles (sliced), 1 tablespoon mustard, 2 tablespoons olive oil, salt, and pepper to taste

Instructions:

1. Spread mustard on each beef slice, then layer with bacon, onion, and pickle.
2. Roll up tightly and secure with toothpicks.
3. Preheat your air fryer to 180°C (350°F).
4. Brush the rouladen with olive oil and season with salt and pepper.
5. Air fry for 20-25 minutes, turning halfway through, until browned and cooked through.

Nutritional info (per serving): Calories: 400 | Fat: 30g | Carbs: 2g | Protein: 30g

Air Fryer Function: Air fry setting for even cooking and crispiness.

Keto Air Fryer Mongolian Beef

Prep: 10 mins | Cook: 15 mins | Serves: 4

Ingredients:

- ✓ US: 500g flank steak (thinly sliced), 2 tablespoons soy sauce, 1 tablespoon sesame oil, 1 tablespoon erythritol, 1 teaspoon garlic powder, 1 teaspoon ginger powder, salt and pepper to taste
- ✓ UK: 500g flank steak (thinly sliced), 2 tablespoons soy sauce, 1 tablespoon sesame oil, 1 tablespoon erythritol, 1 teaspoon garlic powder, 1 teaspoon ginger powder, salt and pepper to taste

Instructions:

1. Preheat your air fryer to 200°C (390°F).
2. Toss the steak slices with soy sauce, sesame oil, erythritol, garlic powder, ginger powder, salt, and pepper.
3. Air fry for 12-15 minutes, shaking halfway, until crispy and caramelised.
4. Serve with a side of keto cauliflower rice.

Nutritional info (per serving): Calories: 300 | Fat: 20g | Carbs: 2g | Protein: 25g

Air Fryer Function: Air fry setting for quick cooking and caramelisation of the beef.

Keto Air Fryer Stuffed Peppers

Prep: 15 mins | Cook: 18 mins |Serves: 4

Ingredients:

- ✓ US: 4 bell peppers (halved and seeds removed), 400g ground beef, 1 onion (chopped), 100g cheddar cheese (shredded), 2 tablespoons olive oil, salt and pepper to taste
- ✓ UK: 4 bell peppers (halved and seeds removed), 400g ground beef, 1 onion (chopped), 100g cheddar cheese (shredded), 2 tablespoons olive oil, salt and pepper to taste

Instructions:

1. Preheat your air fryer to 180°C (350°F).
2. Cook the ground beef and onion in a pan until browned, then stir in salt and pepper.
3. Stuff the bell pepper halves with the beef mixture and top with shredded cheese.
4. Air fry the stuffed peppers for 15-18 minutes, until the peppers are tender and the cheese is melted and golden.

Nutritional info (per serving): Calories: 320 | Fat: 25g | Carbs: 5g | Protein: 20g

Air Fryer Function: Air fry setting for perfectly roasted peppers and melted cheese.

Keto Air Fryer Philly Cheesesteak

Prep: 10 mins | Cook: 10 mins | Serves: 4

Ingredients:

- ✓ US: 500g ribeye steak (thinly sliced), 1 green pepper (sliced), 1 onion (sliced), 100g provolone cheese, 2 tablespoons olive oil, salt and pepper to taste
- ✓ UK: 500g ribeye steak (thinly sliced), 1 green pepper (sliced), 1 onion (sliced), 100g provolone cheese, 2 tablespoons olive oil, salt and pepper to taste

Instructions:

1. Preheat your air fryer to 200°C (390°F).
2. Toss the steak slices, pepper, and onion with olive oil, salt, and pepper.
3. Air fry for 8-10 minutes, stirring halfway through, until the steak is cooked and the veggies are tender.
4. Top with provolone cheese and air fry for another 2 minutes until melted.
5. Serve on keto-friendly rolls or over lettuce.

Nutritional info (per serving): Calories: 350 | Fat: 28g | Carbs: 4g | Protein: 22g

Air Fryer Function: Air fry setting for quick cooking and melting the cheese.

Keto Air Fryer Brisket

Prep: 10 mins | Cook: 2 hours | Serves: 6

Ingredients:

- ✓ US: 1.5kg beef brisket, 2 tablespoons olive oil, 1 tablespoon smoked paprika, 1 teaspoon garlic powder, 1 teaspoon onion powder, salt and pepper to taste
- ✓ UK: 1.5kg beef brisket, 2 tablespoons olive oil, 1 tablespoon smoked paprika, 1 teaspoon garlic powder, 1 teaspoon onion powder, salt and pepper to taste

Instructions:

1. Preheat your air fryer to 160°C (320°F).
2. Rub the brisket with olive oil, smoked paprika, garlic powder, onion powder, salt, and pepper.
3. Place the brisket in the air fryer and cook for 2 hours, turning halfway through, until tender and juicy.
4. Let the brisket rest for 10 minutes before slicing.

Nutritional info (per serving): Calories: 550 | Fat: 40g | Carbs: 2g | Protein: 45g

Air Fryer Function: Roast setting for a slow, even cook and tender meat.

Keto Air Fryer Salmon (3 Ways)

Prep: 5 mins | Cook: 10 mins | Serves: 2

Ingredients:

- ✓ US: 2 salmon fillets (approx. 200g each), 1 tablespoon olive oil, 1 teaspoon garlic powder, 1 teaspoon lemon zest, salt and pepper to taste
- ✓ UK: 2 salmon fillets (approx. 200g each), 1 tablespoon olive oil, 1 teaspoon garlic powder, 1 teaspoon lemon zest, salt and pepper to taste

Instructions:

1. Preheat your air fryer to 180°C (350°F).
2. Brush salmon fillets with olive oil and season with garlic powder, lemon zest, salt, and pepper.
3. Place the fillets in the air fryer basket, skin-side down.
4. Air fry for 8-10 minutes, depending on thickness, until the salmon is cooked through and flakes easily with a fork.

Nutritional info (per serving): Calories: 300 | Fat: 20g | Carbs: 1g | Protein: 25g

Air Fryer Function: Air fry setting for even cooking and crispy skin.

Keto Air Fryer Fish Sticks

Prep: 10 mins | Cook: 12 mins | Serves: 4

Ingredients:

- ✓ US: 400g white fish fillets (cut into strips), 100g almond flour, 50g grated parmesan, 2 eggs (beaten), 1 teaspoon smoked paprika, salt and pepper to taste
- ✓ UK: 400g white fish fillets (cut into strips), 100g almond flour, 50g grated parmesan, 2 eggs (beaten), 1 teaspoon smoked paprika, salt and pepper to taste

Instructions:

1. Preheat your air fryer to 200°C (390°F).
2. In one bowl, mix the almond flour, parmesan, paprika, salt, and pepper.
3. Dip each fish strip into the beaten egg, then coat in the almond flour mixture.
4. Place the fish sticks in the air fryer basket in a single layer.
5. Air fry for 10-12 minutes, flipping halfway through, until golden and crispy.

Nutritional info (per serving): Calories: 280 | Fat: 18g | Carbs: 5g | Protein: 22g

Air Fryer Function: Air fry setting for crispy fish sticks without the need for deep frying.

Keto Air Fryer Coconut Shrimp

Prep: 10 mins | Cook: 8 mins | Serves: 4

Ingredients:

- ✓ US: 500g shrimp (peeled and deveined), 100g shredded coconut, 50g almond flour, 2 eggs (beaten), 1 teaspoon garlic powder, salt and pepper to taste
- ✓ UK: 500g shrimp (peeled and deveined), 100g shredded coconut, 50g almond flour, 2 eggs (beaten), 1 teaspoon garlic powder, salt and pepper to taste

Instructions:

1. Preheat your air fryer to 190°C (375°F).
2. In one bowl, mix the shredded coconut, almond flour, garlic powder, salt, and pepper.
3. Dip each shrimp into the beaten egg, then coat in the coconut mixture.
4. Arrange the shrimp in the air fryer basket in a single layer.
5. Air fry for 6-8 minutes, flipping halfway through, until the shrimp are golden and crispy.

Nutritional info (per serving): Calories: 320 | Fat: 22g | Carbs: 6g | Protein: 23g

Air Fryer Function: Air fry setting for crispy, coconut-coated shrimp without frying.

Keto Air Fryer Lemon Pepper Cod

Prep: 5 mins | Cook: 10 mins | Serves: 2

Ingredients:

- ✓ US: 2 cod fillets (approx. 150g each), 1 tablespoon olive oil, 1 teaspoon lemon pepper seasoning, 1 teaspoon lemon zest, salt to taste
- ✓ UK: 2 cod fillets (approx. 150g each), 1 tablespoon olive oil, 1 teaspoon lemon pepper seasoning, 1 teaspoon lemon zest, salt to taste

Instructions:

1. Preheat your air fryer to 180°C (350°F).
2. Brush the cod fillets with olive oil and season with lemon pepper, lemon zest, and a pinch of salt.
3. Place the fillets in the air fryer basket.
4. Air fry for 8-10 minutes, until the fish is opaque and flakes easily with a fork.

Nutritional info (per serving): Calories: 180 | Fat: 9g | Carbs: 1g | Protein: 23g

Air Fryer Function: Air fry setting for perfectly flaky and seasoned cod.

Keto Air Fryer Cajun Catfish

Prep: 5 mins | Cook: 12 mins | Serves: 2

Ingredients:

- ✓ US: 2 catfish fillets (approx. 180g each), 1 tablespoon Cajun seasoning, 1 tablespoon olive oil
- ✓ UK: 2 catfish fillets (approx. 180g each), 1 tablespoon Cajun seasoning, 1 tablespoon olive oil

Instructions:

1. Preheat your air fryer to 200°C (390°F).
2. Rub the catfish fillets with olive oil and Cajun seasoning.
3. Place the fillets in the air fryer basket.
4. Air fry for 10-12 minutes, flipping halfway through, until the fish is crispy on the outside and cooked through.

Nutritional info (per serving): Calories: 240 | Fat: 14g | Carbs: 2g | Protein: 25g

Air Fryer Function: Air fry setting for a crispy, Cajun-spiced crust.

Keto Air Fryer Garlic Butter Scallops

Prep: 5 mins | Cook: 8 mins | Serves: 4

Ingredients:

- ✓ US: 500g scallops, 2 tablespoons butter (melted), 1 teaspoon garlic powder, salt and pepper to taste
- ✓ UK: 500g scallops, 2 tablespoons butter (melted), 1 teaspoon garlic powder, salt and pepper to taste

Instructions:

1. Preheat your air fryer to 180°C (350°F).
2. Toss the scallops in melted butter, garlic powder, salt, and pepper.
3. Place the scallops in the air fryer basket.
4. Air fry for 6-8 minutes, until the scallops are golden and tender.

Nutritional info (per serving): Calories: 210 | Fat: 12g | Carbs: 2g | Protein: 22g

Air Fryer Function: Air fry setting for perfectly cooked, tender scallops.

Keto Air Fryer Lemon Garlic Shrimp

Prep: 5 mins | Cook: 7 mins | Serves: 4

Ingredients:

- ✓ US: 500g shrimp (peeled and deveined), 2 tablespoons olive oil, 1 teaspoon garlic powder, 1 teaspoon lemon zest, salt and pepper to taste
- ✓ UK: 500g shrimp (peeled and deveined), 2 tablespoons olive oil, 1 teaspoon garlic powder, 1 teaspoon lemon zest, salt and pepper to taste

Instructions:

1. Preheat your air fryer to 190°C (375°F).
2. Toss the shrimp with olive oil, garlic powder, lemon zest, salt, and pepper.
3. Place the shrimp in the air fryer basket in a single layer.
4. Air fry for 5-7 minutes, flipping halfway through, until the shrimp are pink and cooked through.

Nutritional info (per serving): Calories: 210 | Fat: 14g | Carbs: 1g | Protein: 18g

Air Fryer Function: Air fry setting for quick-cooking and perfectly seasoned shrimp.

Keto Air Fryer Blackened Tilapia

Prep: 5 mins | Cook: 10 mins | Serves: 2

Ingredients:

- ✓ US: 2 tilapia fillets (approx. 150g each), 1 tablespoon olive oil, 1 tablespoon Cajun seasoning, salt and pepper to taste
- ✓ UK: 2 tilapia fillets (approx. 150g each), 1 tablespoon olive oil, 1 tablespoon Cajun seasoning, salt and pepper to taste

Instructions:

1. Preheat your air fryer to 180°C (350°F).
2. Rub the tilapia fillets with olive oil, Cajun seasoning, salt, and pepper.
3. Place the fillets in the air fryer basket.
4. Air fry for 8-10 minutes, until the fish is opaque and flakes easily.

Nutritional info (per serving): Calories: 180 | Fat: 9g | Carbs: 2g | Protein: 22g

Air Fryer Function: Air fry setting for quick and crispy tilapia.

Keto Air Fryer Cajun Shrimp

Prep: 5 mins | Cook: 7 mins | Serves: 4

Ingredients:

- ✓ US: 500g shrimp (peeled and deveined), 1 tablespoon Cajun seasoning, 1 tablespoon olive oil
- ✓ UK: 500g shrimp (peeled and deveined), 1 tablespoon Cajun seasoning, 1 tablespoon olive oil

Instructions:

1. Preheat your air fryer to 190°C (375°F).
2. Toss the shrimp with Cajun seasoning and olive oil.
3. Place the shrimp in the air fryer basket.
4. Air fry for 5-7 minutes, until the shrimp are pink and cooked through.

Nutritional info (per serving): Calories: 190 | Fat: 12g | Carbs: 1g | Protein: 20g

Air Fryer Function: Air fry setting for Cajun-spiced shrimp in minutes.

Keto Air Fryer Seafood Medley

Prep: 5 mins | Cook: 12 mins | Serves: 4

Ingredients:

- ✓ US: 200g shrimp (peeled and deveined), 200g scallops, 200g squid rings, 2 tablespoons olive oil, 1 teaspoon garlic powder, salt and pepper to taste
- ✓ UK: 200g shrimp (peeled and deveined), 200g scallops, 200g squid rings, 2 tablespoons olive oil, 1 teaspoon garlic powder, salt and pepper to taste

Instructions:

1. Preheat your air fryer to 190°C (375°F).
2. Toss the seafood with olive oil, garlic powder, salt, and pepper.
3. Place the seafood medley in the air fryer basket in a single layer.
4. Air fry for 10-12 minutes, flipping halfway through, until the seafood is cooked through and tender.

Nutritional info (per serving): Calories: 230 | Fat: 15g | Carbs: 2g | Protein: 21g

Air Fryer Function: Air fry setting for perfectly cooked seafood mix.

Keto Air Fryer Brussels Sprouts

Prep: 5 mins | Cook: 12 mins | Serves: 4

Ingredients:

- ✓ US: 500g Brussels sprouts (halved), 2 tablespoons olive oil, 1 teaspoon garlic powder, 1 tablespoon balsamic vinegar, salt and pepper to taste
- ✓ UK: 500g Brussels sprouts (halved), 2 tablespoons olive oil, 1 teaspoon garlic powder, 1 tablespoon balsamic vinegar, salt and pepper to taste

Instructions:

1. Preheat your air fryer to 190°C (375°F).
2. In a large bowl, toss the Brussels sprouts with olive oil, garlic powder, salt, and pepper.
3. Place the Brussels sprouts in the air fryer basket in a single layer.
4. Air fry for 10-12 minutes, shaking the basket halfway through to ensure even cooking.
5. Once golden and crispy, drizzle with balsamic vinegar and give them a good toss before serving.

Nutritional info (per serving): Calories: 110 | Fat: 9g | Carbs: 8g | Protein: 3g

Air Fryer Function: Air fry setting for crispy and tender Brussels sprouts.

Keto Air Fryer Asparagus (4 Ways)

Prep: 5 mins | Cook: 8 mins | Serves: 4

Ingredients (Basic):

- ✓ US: 400g asparagus, 2 tablespoons olive oil, salt and pepper to taste
- ✓ UK: 400g asparagus, 2 tablespoons olive oil, salt and pepper to taste

Instructions:

1. Preheat your air fryer to 190°C (375°F).
2. Toss the asparagus with olive oil, salt, and pepper.
3. Place the asparagus spears in the air fryer basket in a single layer.
4. Air fry for 6-8 minutes, shaking the basket halfway through.
5. Serve immediately, garnished with parmesan, garlic butter, lemon zest, or balsamic glaze for different flavour twists.

Nutritional info (per serving): Calories: 80 | Fat: 7g | Carbs: 3g | Protein: 2g

Air Fryer Function: Air fry setting for perfectly roasted asparagus.

Keto Air Fryer Green Beans

Prep: 5 mins | Cook: 8 mins | Serves: 4

Ingredients:

- ✓ US: 400g green beans (trimmed), 2 tablespoons olive oil, 1 teaspoon garlic powder, salt and pepper to taste
- ✓ UK: 400g green beans (trimmed), 2 tablespoons olive oil, 1 teaspoon garlic powder, salt and pepper to taste

Instructions:

1. Preheat your air fryer to 190°C (375°F).
2. In a bowl, toss the green beans with olive oil, garlic powder, salt, and pepper.
3. Place them in the air fryer basket.
4. Air fry for 6-8 minutes, shaking the basket halfway through, until they are tender and slightly crisp.

Nutritional info (per serving): Calories: 70 | Fat: 6g | Carbs: 5g | Protein: 2g

Air Fryer Function: Air fry setting for crispy, garlicky green beans.

Keto Air Fryer Cauliflower Wings

Prep: 10 mins | Cook: 15 mins | Serves: 4

Ingredients:

- ✓ US: 1 medium cauliflower (cut into florets), 100g almond flour, 2 eggs (beaten), 1 teaspoon paprika, ½ teaspoon garlic powder, 1 teaspoon salt, 50ml hot sauce
- ✓ UK: 1 medium cauliflower (cut into florets), 100g almond flour, 2 eggs (beaten), 1 teaspoon paprika, ½ teaspoon garlic powder, 1 teaspoon salt, 50ml hot sauce

Instructions:

1. Preheat your air fryer to 200°C (390°F).
2. Toss the cauliflower florets in the beaten eggs.
3. In a separate bowl, combine the almond flour, paprika, garlic powder, and salt.
4. Coat the cauliflower in the almond flour mixture.
5. Place in the air fryer basket and air fry for 12-15 minutes, shaking halfway through.
6. Toss the cooked cauliflower in hot sauce before serving.

Nutritional info (per serving): Calories: 140 | Fat: 9g | Carbs: 9g | Protein: 5g

Air Fryer Function: Air fry setting for crispy, coated cauliflower wings.

Keto Air Fryer Broccoli

Prep: 5 mins | Cook: 8 mins | Serves: 4

Ingredients:

- ✓ US: 400g broccoli florets, 2 tablespoons olive oil, 1 teaspoon garlic powder, 1 teaspoon lemon zest, salt and pepper to taste
- ✓ UK: 400g broccoli florets, 2 tablespoons olive oil, 1 teaspoon garlic powder, 1 teaspoon lemon zest, salt and pepper to taste

Instructions:

1. Preheat your air fryer to 190°C (375°F).
2. Toss the broccoli florets with olive oil, garlic powder, lemon zest, salt, and pepper.
3. Place them in the air fryer basket.
4. Air fry for 6-8 minutes, shaking halfway through.

Nutritional info (per serving): Calories: 100 | Fat: 7g | Carbs: 6g | Protein: 3g

Air Fryer Function: Air fry setting for a crispy-tender broccoli side dish.

Keto Air Fryer Zucchini Fries (3 Ways)

Prep: 10 mins | Cook: 10 mins | Serves: 4

Ingredients (Basic):

- ✓ US: 2 medium zucchinis (cut into fries), 100g almond flour, 2 eggs (beaten), 50g parmesan (grated), salt and pepper to taste
- ✓ UK: 2 medium courgettes (cut into fries), 100g almond flour, 2 eggs (beaten), 50g parmesan (grated), salt and pepper to taste

Instructions:

1. Preheat your air fryer to 200°C (390°F).
2. Dip the zucchini fries into the beaten eggs, then coat them in a mixture of almond flour, parmesan, salt, and pepper.
3. Place the fries in a single layer in the air fryer basket.
4. Air fry for 8-10 minutes, flipping halfway through, until crispy and golden.
5. Serve with garlic aioli, marinara, or ranch dressing for variety.

Nutritional info (per serving): Calories: 140 | Fat: 10g | Carbs: 4g | Protein: 6g

Air Fryer Function: Air fry setting for perfectly crisp zucchini fries.

Keto Air Fryer Roasted Carrots

Prep: 5 mins | Cook: 12 mins | Serves: 4

Ingredients:

- ✓ US: 500g carrots (peeled and sliced), 2 tablespoons olive oil, 1 teaspoon cumin, 1 teaspoon smoked paprika, salt and pepper to taste
- ✓ UK: 500g carrots (peeled and sliced), 2 tablespoons olive oil, 1 teaspoon cumin, 1 teaspoon smoked paprika, salt and pepper to taste

Instructions:

1. Preheat your air fryer to 190°C (375°F).
2. Toss the carrots with olive oil, cumin, smoked paprika, salt, and pepper.
3. Place the carrots in the air fryer basket.
4. Air fry for 10-12 minutes, shaking halfway through, until tender and slightly caramelised.

Nutritional info (per serving): Calories: 120 | Fat: 8g | Carbs: 10g | Protein: 1g

Air Fryer Function: Air fry setting for evenly roasted and flavourful carrots.

Keto Air Fryer Roasted Beets

Prep: 5 mins | Cook: 18 mins | Serves: 4

Ingredients:

- ✓ US: 500g beets (peeled and cubed), 2 tablespoons olive oil, 1 teaspoon thyme, salt and pepper to taste
- ✓ UK: 500g beetroot (peeled and cubed), 2 tablespoons olive oil, 1 teaspoon thyme, salt and pepper to taste

Instructions:

1. Preheat your air fryer to 200°C (390°F).
2. Toss the beet cubes with olive oil, thyme, salt, and pepper.
3. Place them in the air fryer basket.
4. Air fry for 15-18 minutes, shaking halfway through, until tender.

Nutritional info (per serving): Calories: 110 | Fat: 7g | Carbs: 12g | Protein: 2g

Air Fryer Function: Air fry setting for perfectly roasted beets with minimal effort.

Keto Air Fryer Cauliflower Rice (4 Ways)

Prep: 5 mins | Cook: 8 mins | Serves: 4

Ingredients:

- ✓ US: 500g cauliflower (riced), 1 tablespoon olive oil, salt and pepper to taste
- ✓ UK: 500g cauliflower (riced), 1 tablespoon olive oil, salt and pepper to taste

Instructions:

1. Preheat your air fryer to 190°C (375°F).
2. Toss the cauliflower rice with olive oil, salt, and pepper.
3. Place in the air fryer basket and cook for 6-8 minutes, shaking halfway through.
4. Serve plain or flavour with garlic, turmeric, lemon zest, or coconut milk for variety.

Nutritional info (per serving): Calories: 50 | Fat: 3g | Carbs: 3g | Protein: 2g

Air Fryer Function: Air fry setting for light and fluffy cauliflower rice.

Keto Air Fryer Crispy Okra

Prep: 10 mins | Cook: 10 mins | Serves: 4

Ingredients:

- ✓ US: 400g okra (sliced), 2 tablespoons olive oil, 50g almond flour, 1 teaspoon smoked paprika, salt and pepper to taste
- ✓ UK: 400g okra (sliced), 2 tablespoons olive oil, 50g almond flour, 1 teaspoon smoked paprika, salt and pepper to taste

Instructions:

1. Preheat your air fryer to 200°C (390°F).
2. Toss the okra slices with olive oil, almond flour, smoked paprika, salt, and pepper.
3. Place the okra in the air fryer basket.
4. Air fry for 8-10 minutes, shaking halfway through, until crispy.

Nutritional info (per serving): Calories: 120 | Fat: 9g | Carbs: 6g | Protein: 3g

Air Fryer Function: Air fry setting for crispy and flavourful okra fries.

Keto Buffalo Cauliflower Bites

Prep: 10 mins | Cook: 12 mins | Serves: 4

Ingredients:

- ✓ US: 500g cauliflower (cut into florets), 60ml olive oil, 100g almond flour, 1 teaspoon garlic powder, 1 teaspoon onion powder, 120ml buffalo sauce, salt and pepper to taste
- ✓ UK: 500g cauliflower (cut into florets), 60ml olive oil, 100g almond flour, 1 teaspoon garlic powder, 1 teaspoon onion powder, 120ml buffalo sauce, salt and pepper to taste

Instructions:

1. Preheat your air fryer to 200°C (390°F).
2. In a large bowl, combine the cauliflower florets, olive oil, almond flour, garlic powder, onion powder, salt, and pepper. Toss until evenly coated.
3. Place the cauliflower in the air fryer basket in a single layer.
4. Air fry for 10-12 minutes, shaking the basket halfway through.
5. Remove from the air fryer and toss in buffalo sauce. Serve hot.

Nutritional info (per serving): Calories: 120 | Fat: 9g | Carbs: 6g | Protein: 3g

Air Fryer Function: Air fry setting for crispy, flavourful bites.

Keto Mozzarella Sticks

Prep: 10 mins | Cook: 8 mins | Serves: 4

Ingredients:

- ✓ US: 200g mozzarella cheese (cut into sticks), 100g almond flour, 2 eggs (beaten), 50g parmesan cheese (grated), 1 teaspoon Italian seasoning, salt and pepper to taste
- ✓ UK: 200g mozzarella cheese (cut into sticks), 100g almond flour, 2 eggs (beaten), 50g parmesan cheese (grated), 1 teaspoon Italian seasoning, salt and pepper to taste

Instructions:

1. Preheat your air fryer to 200°C (390°F).
2. Set up a breading station with one bowl for the almond flour, one for the beaten eggs, and one for the parmesan cheese mixed with Italian seasoning, salt, and pepper.
3. Dip each mozzarella stick first in almond flour, then in the egg, and finally in the parmesan mixture, ensuring it's well coated.
4. Place the sticks in the air fryer basket.
5. Air fry for 6-8 minutes, until golden brown.

Nutritional info (per serving): Calories: 220 | Fat: 18g | Carbs: 4g | Protein: 12g

Air Fryer Function: Air fry setting for a crispy, gooey cheese experience.

Keto Fried Pickles

Prep: 5 mins | Cook: 10 mins | Serves: 4

Ingredients:

- ✓ US: 300g dill pickle slices, 60g almond flour, 1 egg (beaten), 1 teaspoon garlic powder, 1 teaspoon paprika, salt and pepper to taste
- ✓ UK: 300g dill pickle slices, 60g almond flour, 1 egg (beaten), 1 teaspoon garlic powder, 1 teaspoon paprika, salt and pepper to taste

Instructions:

1. Preheat your air fryer to 200°C (390°F).
2. Pat the pickle slices dry with paper towels.
3. Dip each pickle slice in the beaten egg, then coat with almond flour mixed with garlic powder, paprika, salt, and pepper.
4. Place the pickles in the air fryer basket in a single layer.
5. Air fry for 8-10 minutes, flipping halfway through.

Nutritional info (per serving): Calories: 130 | Fat: 8g | Carbs: 4g | Protein: 5g

Air Fryer Function: Air fry setting for crispy, tangy bites.

Keto Fried Mushrooms

Prep: 10 mins | Cook: 10 mins | Serves: 4

Ingredients:

- ✓ US: 400g mushrooms (whole or halved), 60g almond flour, 1 egg (beaten), 1 teaspoon garlic powder, 1 teaspoon Italian seasoning, salt and pepper to taste
- ✓ UK: 400g mushrooms (whole or halved), 60g almond flour, 1 egg (beaten), 1 teaspoon garlic powder, 1 teaspoon Italian seasoning, salt and pepper to taste

Instructions:

1. Preheat your air fryer to 200°C (390°F).
2. Dip each mushroom in the beaten egg, then coat with almond flour mixed with garlic powder, Italian seasoning, salt, and pepper.
3. Place the mushrooms in the air fryer basket in a single layer.
4. Air fry for 8-10 minutes, until golden and crispy.

Nutritional info (per serving): Calories: 110 | Fat: 6g | Carbs: 8g | Protein: 4g

Air Fryer Function: Air fry setting for crunchy and flavourful mushrooms.

Keto Fried Zucchini

Prep: 10 mins | Cook: 10 mins | Serves: 4

Ingredients:

- ✓ US: 2 medium zucchinis (sliced into rounds), 100g almond flour, 1 egg (beaten), 50g parmesan cheese (grated), 1 teaspoon Italian seasoning, salt and pepper to taste
- ✓ UK: 2 medium courgettes (sliced into rounds), 100g almond flour, 1 egg (beaten), 50g parmesan cheese (grated), 1 teaspoon Italian seasoning, salt and pepper to taste

Instructions:

1. Preheat your air fryer to 200°C (390°F).
2. Dip each zucchini slice in the beaten egg, then coat with a mixture of almond flour, parmesan, Italian seasoning, salt, and pepper.
3. Arrange the coated zucchini in the air fryer basket.
4. Air fry for 8-10 minutes, until crispy and golden.

Nutritional info (per serving): Calories: 140 | Fat: 10g | Carbs: 6g | Protein: 5g

Air Fryer Function: Air fry setting for crunchy, cheesy zucchini bites.

Keto Fried Green Tomatoes

Prep: 10 mins | Cook: 8 mins | Serves: 4

Ingredients:

- ✓ US: 300g green tomatoes (sliced), 60g almond flour, 1 egg (beaten), 1 teaspoon paprika, 1 teaspoon garlic powder, salt and pepper to taste
- ✓ UK: 300g green tomatoes (sliced), 60g almond flour, 1 egg (beaten), 1 teaspoon paprika, 1 teaspoon garlic powder, salt and pepper to taste

Instructions:

1. Preheat your air fryer to 200°C (390°F).
2. Dip each tomato slice in the beaten egg, then coat with almond flour mixed with paprika, garlic powder, salt, and pepper.
3. Place the tomato slices in the air fryer basket.
4. Air fry for 6-8 minutes, flipping halfway through, until golden.

Nutritional info (per serving): Calories: 110 | Fat: 8g | Carbs: 5g | Protein: 2g

Air Fryer Function: Air fry setting for crispy, tangy green tomatoes.

Keto Savory Chickpea Bites

Prep: 10 mins | Cook: 15 mins | Serves: 4

Ingredients:

- ✓ US: 400g canned chickpeas (drained and rinsed), 2 tablespoons olive oil, 1 teaspoon garlic powder, 1 teaspoon cumin, 1 teaspoon paprika, salt and pepper to taste
- ✓ UK: 400g canned chickpeas (drained and rinsed), 2 tablespoons olive oil, 1 teaspoon garlic powder, 1 teaspoon cumin, 1 teaspoon paprika, salt and pepper to taste

Instructions:

1. Preheat your air fryer to 200°C (390°F).
2. In a bowl, toss the chickpeas with olive oil, garlic powder, cumin, paprika, salt, and pepper.
3. Spread the chickpeas in the air fryer basket in a single layer.
4. Air fry for 12-15 minutes, shaking the basket halfway through, until crispy.

Nutritional info (per serving): Calories: 180 | Fat: 6g | Carbs: 24g | Protein: 8g

Air Fryer Function: Air fry setting for crunchy, savoury bites.

Keto Pesto Parmesan Crisps

Prep: 5 mins | Cook: 5 mins | Serves: 4

Ingredients:

- ✓ US: 100g grated parmesan cheese, 2 tablespoons pesto, 1 teaspoon Italian seasoning
- ✓ UK: 100g grated parmesan cheese, 2 tablespoons pesto, 1 teaspoon Italian seasoning

Instructions:

1. Preheat your air fryer to 200°C (390°F).
2. In a bowl, mix the parmesan cheese, pesto, and Italian seasoning until well combined.
3. Spoon small mounds onto parchment paper in the air fryer basket.
4. Air fry for 4-5 minutes until golden and crispy.

Nutritional info (per serving): Calories: 100 | Fat: 8g | Carbs: 1g | Protein: 8g

Air Fryer Function: Air fry setting for crispy, cheesy bites.

Keto Air Fryer Meatballs

Prep: 10 mins | Cook: 15 mins | Serves: 4

Ingredients:

- ✓ US: 500g ground beef (or turkey), 50g almond flour, 1 egg, 2 tablespoons parsley (chopped), 1 teaspoon garlic powder, salt and pepper to taste
- ✓ UK: 500g ground beef (or turkey), 50g almond flour, 1 egg, 2 tablespoons parsley (chopped), 1 teaspoon garlic powder, salt and pepper to taste

Instructions:

1. Preheat your air fryer to 200°C (390°F).
2. In a large bowl, combine the ground meat, almond flour, egg, parsley, garlic powder, salt, and pepper. Mix until well combined.
3. Form the mixture into small meatballs (about 2.5cm each).
4. Place the meatballs in the air fryer basket.
5. Air fry for 12-15 minutes, until cooked through.

Nutritional info (per serving): Calories: 250 | Fat: 18g | Carbs: 3g | Protein: 22g

Air Fryer Function: Air fry setting for juicy, flavourful meatballs.

Keto Air Fryer Cheesy Spinach Artichoke Cups

Prep: 10 mins | Cook: 10 mins | Serves: 4

Ingredients:

- ✓ US: 200g spinach (cooked and drained), 100g cream cheese, 50g mozzarella cheese (grated), 100g canned artichoke hearts (chopped), 1 teaspoon garlic powder, salt and pepper to taste
- ✓ UK: 200g spinach (cooked and drained), 100g cream cheese, 50g mozzarella cheese (grated), 100g canned artichoke hearts (chopped), 1 teaspoon garlic powder, salt and pepper to taste

Instructions:

1. Preheat your air fryer to 200°C (390°F).
2. In a bowl, combine the spinach, cream cheese, mozzarella, artichoke hearts, garlic powder, salt, and pepper. Mix well.
3. Spoon the mixture into muffin cups or small ramekins.
4. Place in the air fryer basket.
5. Air fry for 8-10 minutes, until bubbly and golden.

Nutritional info (per serving): Calories: 180 | Fat: 15g | Carbs: 5g | Protein: 8g

Air Fryer Function: Air fry setting for warm, cheesy bites.

Keto Bacon and Egg Mini Quiches

Prep: 10 mins | Cook: 15 mins | Serves: 4

Ingredients:

- ✓ US: 4 large eggs, 100ml heavy cream, 150g cooked bacon (chopped), 50g shredded cheese (your choice), salt, pepper, and fresh herbs (optional)
- ✓ UK: 4 large eggs, 100ml double cream, 150g cooked bacon (chopped), 50g grated cheese (your choice), salt, pepper, and fresh herbs (optional)

Instructions:

1. Preheat your air fryer to 180°C (356°F).
2. In a bowl, whisk together the eggs, heavy cream, salt, and pepper until well combined.
3. Stir in the chopped bacon and shredded cheese.
4. Lightly grease muffin tins or silicone cups with cooking spray, and pour the egg mixture evenly into each cup.
5. Place the cups in the air fryer basket and cook for 12-15 minutes or until the quiches are set and lightly golden on top.
6. Let them cool slightly before removing. Serve warm, garnished with fresh herbs if desired.

Nutritional info (per serving): Calories: 210 | Fat: 18g | Carbs: 2g | Protein: 12g

Air Fryer Function: Air fry setting for perfectly cooked mini quiches.

Keto Sausage Patties

Prep: 10 mins | Cook: 10 mins | Serves: 4

Ingredients:

- ✓ US: 500g ground pork (or turkey), 1 teaspoon dried sage, 1 teaspoon garlic powder, 1 teaspoon onion powder, 1 teaspoon salt, 1/2 teaspoon black pepper
- ✓ UK: 500g minced pork (or turkey), 1 teaspoon dried sage, 1 teaspoon garlic powder, 1 teaspoon onion powder, 1 teaspoon salt, 1/2 teaspoon black pepper

Instructions:

1. Preheat your air fryer to 200°C (390°F).
2. In a bowl, mix the ground pork, sage, garlic powder, onion powder, salt, and pepper until well combined.
3. Form the mixture into small patties (about 5cm wide).
4. Place the patties in the air fryer basket in a single layer.
5. Cook for 8-10 minutes, flipping halfway through, until cooked through and browned.

Nutritional info (per serving): Calories: 230 | Fat: 18g | Carbs: 0g | Protein: 22g

Air Fryer Function: Air fry setting for juicy and flavourful sausage patties.

Keto Air Fryer Pancakes

Prep: 5 mins | Cook: 10 mins | Serves: 2

Ingredients:

- ✓ US: 100g almond flour, 2 large eggs, 30ml almond milk, 1 teaspoon baking powder, 1 teaspoon vanilla extract, sweetener to taste
- ✓ UK: 100g almond flour, 2 large eggs, 30ml almond milk, 1 teaspoon baking powder, 1 teaspoon vanilla extract, sweetener to taste

Instructions:

1. Preheat your air fryer to 180°C (356°F).
2. In a bowl, mix the almond flour, eggs, almond milk, baking powder, vanilla extract, and sweetener until smooth.
3. Pour the batter into a silicone pancake mold, filling each cavity halfway.
4. Place the mold in the air fryer basket and cook for 8-10 minutes, until the pancakes are set.
5. Remove and let cool slightly before serving with your choice of toppings.

Nutritional info (per serving): Calories: 250 | Fat: 18g | Carbs: 6g | Protein: 10g

Air Fryer Function: Air fry setting for fluffy pancakes with a lovely texture.

Keto Cinnamon Roll Bites (3 Ways)

Prep: 10 mins | Cook: 10 mins | Serves: 4

Ingredients (Base):

- ✓ US: 100g almond flour, 1 teaspoon baking powder, 2 large eggs, 30ml almond milk, 1 teaspoon vanilla extract, sweetener to taste
- ✓ UK: 100g almond flour, 1 teaspoon baking powder, 2 large eggs, 30ml almond milk, 1 teaspoon vanilla extract, sweetener to taste

Cinnamon Sugar Filling (Option 1):

- ✓ US: 30g butter (melted), 1 tablespoon cinnamon, 1 tablespoon sweetener
- ✓ UK: 30g butter (melted), 1 tablespoon cinnamon, 1 tablespoon sweetener

Chocolate Hazelnut Filling (Option 2):

- ✓ US: 30g sugar-free chocolate hazelnut spread
- ✓ UK: 30g sugar-free chocolate hazelnut spread

Instructions:

1. Preheat your air fryer to 180°C (356°F).
2. In a bowl, mix the almond flour, baking powder, eggs, almond milk, vanilla extract, and sweetener until smooth.
3. For the cinnamon sugar filling, mix the melted butter, cinnamon, and sweetener in another bowl. For the chocolate filling, set aside the spread.
4. Spread the batter on a piece of parchment paper and sprinkle with your chosen filling. Roll tightly to form a log.
5. Cut into bite-sized pieces and place in the air fryer basket.
6. Cook for 8-10 minutes, until golden and cooked through.

Nutritional info (per serving): Calories: 200 | Fat: 16g | Carbs: 5g | Protein: 6g

Air Fryer Function: Air fry setting for perfectly cooked, gooey bites.

Keto Chaffles (4 Ways)

Prep: 5 mins | Cook: 10 mins | Serves: 2

Ingredients (Base):

- ✓ US: 100g shredded mozzarella cheese, 1 large egg, 30g almond flour (optional), salt and pepper to taste
- ✓ UK: 100g shredded mozzarella cheese, 1 large egg, 30g almond flour (optional), salt and pepper to taste

Instructions:

1. Preheat your air fryer to 200°C (390°F).
2. In a bowl, mix the shredded cheese, egg, almond flour (if using), salt, and pepper until combined.
3. Pour half the mixture into a preheated waffle maker and cook according to manufacturer's instructions (about 3-4 minutes).
4. Alternatively, you can spoon the mixture into a silicone mould in the air fryer basket.
5. Air fry for 6-8 minutes until golden and crispy.

Nutritional info (per serving): Calories: 180 | Fat: 14g | Carbs: 2g | Protein: 10g

Air Fryer Function: Air fry setting for crispy and cheesy chaffles.

Keto Breakfast Bowls (2 Ways)

Prep: 10 mins | Cook: 15 mins | Serves: 2

Ingredients (Base):

- ✓ US: 4 large eggs, 150g spinach (fresh or frozen), 100g cherry tomatoes (halved), 100g cooked bacon (chopped), salt and pepper to taste
- ✓ UK: 4 large eggs, 150g spinach (fresh or frozen), 100g cherry tomatoes (halved), 100g cooked bacon (chopped), salt and pepper to taste

Instructions:

1. Preheat your air fryer to 200°C (390°F).
2. In a bowl, whisk the eggs with salt and pepper.
3. Arrange the spinach, cherry tomatoes, and bacon in a baking dish that fits in your air fryer basket.
4. Pour the egg mixture over the vegetables and bacon.
5. Air fry for 12-15 minutes, until the eggs are set.
6. Remove and serve hot.

Nutritional info (per serving): Calories: 220 | Fat: 16g | Carbs: 5g | Protein: 15g

Air Fryer Function: Air fry setting for fluffy and flavourful breakfast bowls.

Keto Egg Bites (4 Ways)

Prep: 10 mins | Cook: 15 mins | Serves: 4

Ingredients (Base):

- ✓ US: 4 large eggs, 100ml heavy cream, 50g cheese (your choice), salt and pepper to taste
- ✓ UK: 4 large eggs, 100ml double cream, 50g cheese (your choice), salt and pepper to taste

Instructions:

1. Preheat your air fryer to 180°C (356°F).
2. In a bowl, whisk the eggs, cream, salt, and pepper until well mixed.
3. Divide the cheese and any other desired ingredients (like cooked bacon, spinach, or herbs) among the muffin cups.
4. Pour the egg mixture over the fillings until just full.
5. Place the cups in the air fryer basket and cook for 12-15 minutes, or until the egg bites are set.

Nutritional info (per serving): Calories: 210 | Fat: 18g | Carbs: 2g | Protein: 12g

Air Fryer Function: Air fry setting for perfectly cooked egg bites.

Keto Breakfast Casserole

Prep: 10 mins | Cook: 25 mins | Serves: 4

Ingredients:

- ✓ US: 500g ground sausage, 4 large eggs, 100ml heavy cream, 100g shredded cheese, 100g spinach, salt and pepper to taste
- ✓ UK: 500g sausage meat, 4 large eggs, 100ml double cream, 100g grated cheese, 100g spinach, salt and pepper to taste

Instructions:

1. Preheat your air fryer to 180°C (356°F).
2. In a frying pan, cook the sausage until browned. Drain excess fat.
3. In a bowl, whisk together the eggs, cream, salt, and pepper.
4. In a baking dish, layer the sausage, spinach, and cheese, then pour the egg mixture on top.
5. Air fry for 20-25 minutes, until the casserole is set and golden.

Nutritional info (per serving): Calories: 300 | Fat: 25g | Carbs: 3g | Protein: 18g

Air Fryer Function: Air fry setting for a fluffy and hearty breakfast casserole.

Keto Air Fryer Breakfast Tacos

Prep: 10 mins | Cook: 10 mins | Serves: 2

Ingredients:

- ✓ US: 4 large eggs, 100g cooked bacon (chopped), 100g cheese (shredded), 4 lettuce leaves (for wraps), salt and pepper to taste
- ✓ UK: 4 large eggs, 100g cooked bacon (chopped), 100g cheese (grated), 4 lettuce leaves (for wraps), salt and pepper to taste

Instructions:

1. Preheat your air fryer to 200°C (390°F).
2. In a bowl, whisk the eggs with salt and pepper.
3. Pour the egg mixture into a baking dish and air fry for 5-7 minutes until set.
4. Cut the egg into pieces and assemble the tacos by placing the egg, bacon, and cheese in the lettuce leaves.
5. Serve immediately with your favourite salsa or hot sauce.

Nutritional info (per serving): Calories: 250 | Fat: 20g | Carbs: 3g | Protein: 15g

Air Fryer Function: Air fry setting for a quick and easy breakfast.

Keto Air Fryer Sausage and Cheddar Muffins

Prep: 10 mins | Cook: 15 mins | Serves: 6

Ingredients:

- ✓ US: 200g almond flour, 200g cooked sausage (crumbled), 100g cheddar cheese (shredded), 4 large eggs, 1 teaspoon baking powder, salt and pepper to taste
- ✓ UK: 200g almond flour, 200g cooked sausage (crumbled), 100g cheddar cheese (grated), 4 large eggs, 1 teaspoon baking powder, salt and pepper to taste

Instructions:

1. Preheat your air fryer to 180°C (356°F).
2. In a bowl, mix the almond flour, sausage, cheddar, eggs, baking powder, salt, and pepper until well combined.
3. Spoon the mixture into greased muffin tins or silicone cups.
4. Place the cups in the air fryer basket and cook for 12-15 minutes, or until golden and cooked through.
5. Let cool slightly before serving warm.

Nutritional info (per serving): Calories: 220 | Fat: 18g | Carbs: 4g | Protein: 12g

Air Fryer Function: Air fry setting for tasty and satisfying muffins.

Keto Air Fryer Turkey Meatballs (3 Ways)

Prep: 15 mins | Cook: 15 mins | Serves: 4

Ingredients:

- ✓ US: 500g ground turkey, 30g grated Parmesan cheese, 1 large egg, 1 teaspoon garlic powder, 1 teaspoon onion powder, salt, pepper, 30g fresh parsley (chopped)
- ✓ UK: 500g ground turkey, 30g grated Parmesan cheese, 1 large egg, 1 teaspoon garlic powder, 1 teaspoon onion powder, salt, pepper, 30g fresh parsley (chopped)

Instructions:

1. Preheat your air fryer to 200°C (400°F).
2. In a large bowl, combine the ground turkey, Parmesan cheese, egg, garlic powder, onion powder, salt, pepper, and parsley. Mix until well combined.
3. Form the mixture into meatballs, about 2.5 cm (1 inch) in diameter.
4. Place the meatballs in a single layer in the air fryer basket.
5. Cook for 12-15 minutes, flipping halfway through, until the meatballs are golden brown and cooked through.
6. Serve with your favourite keto-friendly dipping sauce.

Nutritional info: Calories: 200 | Fat: 10g | Carbs: 2g | Protein: 24g

Air Fryer Function: Use the air fry setting for quick, even cooking that keeps the meatballs juicy and tender.

Keto Buffalo Chicken Meatballs

Prep: 10 mins | Cook: 15 mins | Serves: 4

Ingredients:

- ✓ US: 500g ground chicken, 50g cream cheese (softened), 30ml hot sauce, 1 teaspoon garlic powder, 1 teaspoon onion powder, salt, pepper
- ✓ UK: 500g ground chicken, 50g cream cheese (softened), 30ml hot sauce, 1 teaspoon garlic powder, 1 teaspoon onion powder, salt, pepper

Instructions:

1. Preheat your air fryer to 200°C (400°F).
2. In a bowl, mix the ground chicken, cream cheese, hot sauce, garlic powder, onion powder, salt, and pepper.
3. Shape the mixture into meatballs.
4. Arrange the meatballs in the air fryer basket.
5. Cook for 12-15 minutes or until they are cooked through and slightly crispy on the outside.
6. Toss the cooked meatballs in extra hot sauce before serving.

Nutritional info: Calories: 210 | Fat: 12g | Carbs: 1g | Protein: 22g

Air Fryer Function: Use the air fry setting for a crispy exterior while keeping the inside moist and flavourful.

Keto Air Fryer Chicken Nuggets (4 Ways)

Prep: 15 mins | Cook: 10 mins | Serves: 4

Ingredients:

- ✓ US: 500g chicken breast (cut into bite-sized pieces), 100g almond flour, 50g grated Parmesan cheese, 2 large eggs, salt, pepper, your choice of spices (paprika, garlic powder, etc.)
- ✓ UK: 500g chicken breast (cut into bite-sized pieces), 100g almond flour, 50g grated Parmesan cheese, 2 large eggs, salt, pepper, your choice of spices (paprika, garlic powder, etc.)

Instructions:

1. Preheat your air fryer to 200°C (400°F).
2. Set up a breading station: In one bowl, whisk the eggs. In another bowl, mix almond flour, Parmesan cheese, salt, pepper, and spices.
3. Dip each chicken piece in the egg, then coat it with the almond flour mixture.
4. Place the breaded chicken nuggets in the air fryer basket.
5. Cook for 8-10 minutes, flipping halfway, until golden brown and cooked through.
6. Serve with your favourite keto-friendly dipping sauces.

Nutritional info: Calories: 250 | Fat: 16g | Carbs: 5g | Protein: 20g

Air Fryer Function: Use the air fry setting for a crunchy texture without the excess oil.

Keto Air Fryer Chicken Tenders (3 Ways)

Prep: 15 mins | Cook: 10 mins | Serves: 4

Ingredients:

- ✓ US: 500g chicken breast (cut into strips), 100g coconut flour, 2 large eggs, 50g grated Parmesan cheese, salt, pepper, garlic powder
- ✓ UK: 500g chicken breast (cut into strips), 100g coconut flour, 2 large eggs, 50g grated Parmesan cheese, salt, pepper, garlic powder

Instructions:

1. Preheat your air fryer to 200°C (400°F).
2. Set up a breading station: In one bowl, beat the eggs. In another bowl, mix coconut flour, Parmesan cheese, salt, pepper, and garlic powder.
3. Dip each chicken strip in the egg, then coat with the coconut flour mixture.
4. Place the chicken tenders in the air fryer basket in a single layer.
5. Cook for 8-10 minutes, flipping halfway, until golden and cooked through.
6. Enjoy with your favourite dipping sauce.

Nutritional info: Calories: 300 | Fat: 18g | Carbs: 7g | Protein: 28g

Air Fryer Function: Use the air fry setting to achieve a crispy, crunchy coating.

Keto Air Fryer Lemon Pepper Chicken

Prep: 10 mins | Cook: 20 mins | Serves: 4

Ingredients:

- ✓ US: 4 chicken thighs (bone-in, skin-on), 30ml olive oil, 1 teaspoon lemon pepper seasoning, salt
- ✓ UK: 4 chicken thighs (bone-in, skin-on), 30ml olive oil, 1 teaspoon lemon pepper seasoning, salt

Instructions:

1. Preheat your air fryer to 200°C (400°F).
2. Rub the chicken thighs with olive oil and season with lemon pepper and salt.
3. Place the chicken thighs in the air fryer basket, skin-side up.
4. Cook for 18-20 minutes, until the skin is crispy and the internal temperature reaches 75°C (165°F).
5. Let the chicken rest for a few minutes before serving.

Nutritional info: Calories: 360 | Fat: 25g | Carbs: 0g | Protein: 35g

Air Fryer Function: Use the air fry setting for an evenly cooked, crispy skin.

Keto Air Fryer Chicken Wings

Prep: 10 mins | Cook: 25 mins | Serves: 4

Ingredients:

- ✓ US: 1kg chicken wings, 30ml olive oil, 1 teaspoon garlic powder, 1 teaspoon onion powder, salt, pepper
- ✓ UK: 1kg chicken wings, 30ml olive oil, 1 teaspoon garlic powder, 1 teaspoon onion powder, salt, pepper

Instructions:

1. Preheat your air fryer to 200°C (400°F).
2. In a large bowl, toss the chicken wings with olive oil, garlic powder, onion powder, salt, and pepper until evenly coated.
3. Arrange the wings in a single layer in the air fryer basket.
4. Cook for 20-25 minutes, flipping halfway, until crispy and golden brown.
5. Serve with a side of low-carb veggies.

Nutritional info: Calories: 400 | Fat: 28g | Carbs: 0g | Protein: 36g

Air Fryer Function: Use the air fry setting to achieve that perfect crispy texture.

Keto Air Fryer Chicken Thighs (4 Ways)

Prep: 10 mins | Cook: 25 mins | Serves: 4

Ingredients:

- ✓ US: 4 chicken thighs (bone-in, skin-on), 30ml olive oil, 1 tablespoon your choice of seasoning (paprika, Italian seasoning, etc.), salt
- ✓ UK: 4 chicken thighs (bone-in, skin-on), 30ml olive oil, 1 tablespoon your choice of seasoning (paprika, Italian seasoning, etc.), salt

Instructions:

1. Preheat your air fryer to 200°C (400°F).
2. Rub the chicken thighs with olive oil and your choice of seasoning and salt.
3. Place the thighs in the air fryer basket skin-side up.
4. Cook for 20-25 minutes or until the internal temperature reaches 75°C (165°F).
5. Let the thighs rest for a few minutes before serving.

Nutritional info: Calories: 360 | Fat: 25g | Carbs: 0g | Protein: 35g

Air Fryer Function: Use the air fry setting to lock in moisture and flavour.

Keto Air Fryer Chicken Drumsticks (3 Ways)

Prep: 10 mins | Cook: 30 mins | Serves: 4

Ingredients:

- ✓ US: 8 chicken drumsticks, 30ml olive oil, 1 teaspoon paprika, 1 teaspoon garlic powder, salt, pepper
- ✓ UK: 8 chicken drumsticks, 30ml olive oil, 1 teaspoon paprika, 1 teaspoon garlic powder, salt, pepper

Instructions:

1. Preheat your air fryer to 200°C (400°F).
2. In a bowl, toss the drumsticks with olive oil, paprika, garlic powder, salt, and pepper until well coated.
3. Place the drumsticks in the air fryer basket in a single layer.
4. Cook for 25-30 minutes, turning halfway, until crispy and cooked through.
5. Serve with your favourite keto dipping sauce.

Nutritional info: Calories: 400 | Fat: 28g | Carbs: 0g | Protein: 38g

Air Fryer Function: Use the air fry setting for crispy skin and juicy meat.

Keto Air Fryer Crispy Fried Chicken

Prep: 15 mins | Cook: 30 mins | Serves: 4

Ingredients:

- ✓ US: 1kg chicken pieces (legs, wings, or breasts), 100g almond flour, 50g coconut flour, 2 large eggs, 30ml buttermilk, salt, pepper, spices (optional)
- ✓ UK: 1kg chicken pieces (legs, wings, or breasts), 100g almond flour, 50g coconut flour, 2 large eggs, 30ml buttermilk, salt, pepper, spices (optional)

Instructions:

1. Preheat your air fryer to 200°C (400°F).
2. In one bowl, whisk the eggs and buttermilk. In another bowl, mix the almond flour, coconut flour, salt, pepper, and spices.
3. Dip each piece of chicken in the egg mixture, then coat with the flour mixture.
4. Arrange the chicken pieces in the air fryer basket.
5. Cook for 25-30 minutes, turning halfway, until golden brown and cooked through.
6. Serve hot with your favourite keto dipping sauces.

Nutritional info: Calories: 450 | Fat: 30g | Carbs: 5g | Protein: 40g

Air Fryer Function: Use the air fry setting to achieve a crunchy, fried texture without the oil.

Keto Air Fryer Chicken Fajitas

Prep: 15 mins | Cook: 15 mins | Serves: 4

Ingredients:

- ✓ US: 500g chicken breast (sliced), 1 bell pepper (sliced), 1 onion (sliced), 30ml olive oil, 1 teaspoon chili powder, 1 teaspoon cumin, salt, pepper
- ✓ UK: 500g chicken breast (sliced), 1 bell pepper (sliced), 1 onion (sliced), 30ml olive oil, 1 teaspoon chili powder, 1 teaspoon cumin, salt, pepper

Instructions:

1. Preheat your air fryer to 200°C (400°F).
2. In a bowl, combine the chicken, bell pepper, onion, olive oil, chili powder, cumin, salt, and pepper. Toss until evenly coated.
3. Place the mixture in the air fryer basket.
4. Cook for 12-15 minutes, shaking the basket halfway through.
5. Serve in lettuce wraps or with low-carb tortillas.

Nutritional info: Calories: 280 | Fat: 14g | Carbs: 5g | Protein: 30g

Air Fryer Function: Use the air fry setting for a quick, healthy meal that locks in flavour and moisture.

Keto Air Fryer Pork Carnitas

Prep: 10 mins | Cook: 45 mins | Serves: 4

Ingredients:

- ✓ US: 500g pork shoulder (cut into chunks), 1 tablespoon olive oil, 1 teaspoon cumin, 1 teaspoon smoked paprika, 1 teaspoon garlic powder, 1/2 teaspoon oregano, juice of 1 lime, salt and pepper to taste
- ✓ UK: 500g pork shoulder (cut into chunks), 1 tablespoon olive oil, 1 teaspoon cumin, 1 teaspoon smoked paprika, 1 teaspoon garlic powder, 1/2 teaspoon oregano, juice of 1 lime, salt and pepper to taste

Instructions:

1. Preheat the air fryer to 200°C (390°F).
2. Toss the pork chunks in olive oil, cumin, smoked paprika, garlic powder, oregano, lime juice, salt, and pepper.
3. Place the pork in the air fryer basket in a single layer.
4. Air fry for 40-45 minutes, shaking the basket every 10 minutes to ensure even cooking.
5. Once crispy and tender, shred the pork with a fork and serve with keto tortillas or lettuce wraps.

Nutritional info: Calories: 330 | Fat: 24g | Carbs: 2g | Protein: 25g

Air Fryer Function: The air fry function crisps the pork to perfection while keeping it juicy inside.

Keto Air Fryer BBQ Ribs

Prep: 10 mins | Cook: 40 mins | Serves: 4

Ingredients:

- ✓ US: 1kg pork ribs (cut into portions), 120ml sugar-free BBQ sauce, 1 tablespoon olive oil, 1 teaspoon smoked paprika, 1 teaspoon garlic powder, salt and pepper to taste
- ✓ UK: 1kg pork ribs (cut into portions), 120ml sugar-free BBQ sauce, 1 tablespoon olive oil, 1 teaspoon smoked paprika, 1 teaspoon garlic powder, salt and pepper to taste

Instructions:

1. Preheat your air fryer to 180°C (355°F).
2. Rub the pork ribs with olive oil, smoked paprika, garlic powder, salt, and pepper.
3. Place the ribs in the air fryer basket in a single layer.
4. Air fry for 30 minutes, flipping halfway through.
5. After 30 minutes, brush the ribs with the sugar-free BBQ sauce.
6. Continue air frying for another 10 minutes until the ribs are caramelised and tender.
7. Serve hot, with extra BBQ sauce on the side for dipping.

Nutritional info: Calories: 420 | Fat: 32g | Carbs: 5g | Protein: 28g

Air Fryer Function: Use the air fry setting for even cooking and crisping the ribs while maintaining juiciness.

Keto Air Fryer Prosciutto-Wrapped Asparagus

Prep: 5 mins | Cook: 10 mins | Serves: 4

Ingredients:

- ✓ US: 12 asparagus spears, 6 slices of prosciutto (halved), 1 tablespoon olive oil, salt and pepper to taste
- ✓ UK: 12 asparagus spears, 6 slices of prosciutto (halved), 1 tablespoon olive oil, salt and pepper to taste

Instructions:

1. Preheat the air fryer to 200°C (390°F).
2. Wrap each asparagus spear with half a slice of prosciutto.
3. Lightly drizzle with olive oil and season with salt and pepper.
4. Place the wrapped asparagus in the air fryer basket in a single layer.
5. Air fry for 8-10 minutes, until the prosciutto is crispy and the asparagus is tender.
6. Serve as a quick and elegant appetiser or side dish.

Nutritional info: Calories: 90 | Fat: 6g | Carbs: 2g | Protein: 6g

Air Fryer Function: The air fry setting crisps the prosciutto perfectly while gently cooking the asparagus.

Keto Air Fryer Pork Egg Rolls (3 Ways)

Prep: 15 mins | Cook: 12 mins | Serves: 4

Ingredients:

- ✓ US: 400g ground pork, 100g cabbage (shredded), 50g carrots (shredded), 1 tablespoon soy sauce (or coconut aminos), 1 teaspoon sesame oil, 1 teaspoon garlic powder, low-carb egg roll wrappers, 1 tablespoon olive oil for brushing
- ✓ UK: 400g ground pork, 100g cabbage (shredded), 50g carrots (shredded), 1 tablespoon soy sauce (or coconut aminos), 1 teaspoon sesame oil, 1 teaspoon garlic powder, low-carb egg roll wrappers, 1 tablespoon olive oil for brushing

Instructions:

1. Preheat the air fryer to 180°C (355°F).
2. In a pan, cook the ground pork with garlic powder, sesame oil, and soy sauce until browned.
3. Stir in the cabbage and carrots, and cook for another 2 minutes. Remove from heat.
4. Spoon the filling into low-carb egg roll wrappers and fold into rolls.
5. Lightly brush each roll with olive oil and place them in the air fryer basket in a single layer.
6. Air fry for 10-12 minutes, flipping halfway, until the rolls are golden and crispy.
7. Serve with keto-friendly dipping sauces.

Nutritional info: Calories: 250 | Fat: 18g | Carbs: 4g | Protein: 16g

Air Fryer Function: The air fry setting crisps up the egg rolls without deep frying, making them healthier and keto-friendly.

Keto Air Fryer Ham Cups with Cheese

Prep: 5 mins | Cook: 10 mins | Serves: 6

Ingredients:

- ✓ US: 6 slices of ham, 6 eggs, 50g cheddar cheese (grated), 1 tablespoon olive oil, salt and pepper to taste
- ✓ UK: 6 slices of ham, 6 eggs, 50g cheddar cheese (grated), 1 tablespoon olive oil, salt and pepper to taste

Instructions:

1. Preheat the air fryer to 180°C (355°F).
2. Lightly grease a muffin tin or use silicone cups.
3. Line each cup with a slice of ham, creating a small "ham cup".
4. Crack an egg into each ham cup and top with grated cheddar.
5. Place the cups into the air fryer basket and cook for 8-10 minutes, until the eggs are set and the cheese is melted.
6. Serve as a keto-friendly breakfast or snack option.

Nutritional info: Calories: 150 | Fat: 11g | Carbs: 1g | Protein: 12g

Air Fryer Function: The bake function works well to evenly cook the eggs and melt the cheese.

Keto Air Fryer Pork Belly Bites

Prep: 10 mins | Cook: 25 mins | Serves: 4

Ingredients:

- ✓ US: 500g pork belly (cut into bite-sized cubes), 1 tablespoon olive oil, 1 teaspoon garlic powder, 1 teaspoon smoked paprika, salt and pepper to taste
- ✓ UK: 500g pork belly (cut into bite-sized cubes), 1 tablespoon olive oil, 1 teaspoon garlic powder, 1 teaspoon smoked paprika, salt and pepper to taste

Instructions:

1. Preheat the air fryer to 200°C (390°F).
2. Toss the pork belly cubes in olive oil, garlic powder, smoked paprika, salt, and pepper.
3. Place the pork belly in the air fryer basket in a single layer.
4. Air fry for 20-25 minutes, shaking the basket halfway through to ensure even cooking.
5. The pork belly should be crispy on the outside and tender on the inside.
6. Serve as a delicious keto snack or appetiser.

Nutritional info: Calories: 320 | Fat: 28g | Carbs: 1g | Protein: 15g

Air Fryer Function: The air fry setting ensures the pork belly bites get perfectly crispy without deep frying.

Keto Air Fryer Sausage Balls

Prep: 10 mins | Cook: 15 mins | Serves: 4

Ingredients:

- ✓ US: 500g ground sausage (pork or turkey), 100g almond flour, 100g cheddar cheese (grated), 1 teaspoon garlic powder, 1 teaspoon onion powder, salt and pepper to taste
- ✓ UK: 500g ground sausage (pork or turkey), 100g almond flour, 100g cheddar cheese (grated), 1 teaspoon garlic powder, 1 teaspoon onion powder, salt and pepper to taste

Instructions:

1. Preheat the air fryer to 190°C (375°F).
2. In a large bowl, combine the sausage, almond flour, grated cheddar, garlic powder, onion powder, salt, and pepper. Mix until well combined.
3. Roll the mixture into small balls and place them in the air fryer basket in a single layer.
4. Air fry for 12-15 minutes, shaking the basket halfway through to ensure even cooking.
5. Serve as a savoury snack or appetiser.

Nutritional info: Calories: 320 | Fat: 28g | Carbs: 2g | Protein: 18g

Air Fryer Function: The air fry setting ensures even cooking, making the sausage balls crispy on the outside and tender on the inside.

Keto Air Fryer Bacon-Wrapped Smokies

Prep: 10 mins | Cook: 12 mins | Serves: 6

Ingredients:

- ✓ US: 12 mini sausages (smokies), 6 slices of bacon (cut in half), 1 tablespoon brown erythritol (optional), toothpicks
- ✓ UK: 12 mini sausages (smokies), 6 slices of bacon (cut in half), 1 tablespoon brown erythritol (optional), toothpicks

Instructions:

1. Preheat the air fryer to 190°C (375°F).
2. Wrap each mini sausage with half a slice of bacon and secure with a toothpick.
3. Optionally, sprinkle the brown erythritol on the wrapped smokies for a sweet twist.
4. Place the wrapped sausages in the air fryer basket in a single layer.
5. Air fry for 10-12 minutes, until the bacon is crispy and the sausages are cooked through.
6. Serve warm as a fun party snack or appetiser.

Nutritional info: Calories: 110 | Fat: 9g | Carbs: 1g | Protein: 5g

Air Fryer Function: Air fry for quick, even cooking and perfectly crisp bacon.

Keto Air Fryer Pork Chops (3 Ways)

Prep: 10 mins | Cook: 20 mins | Serves: 4

Ingredients:

- ✓ US: 4 pork chops (boneless, 1-inch thick), 2 tablespoons olive oil, salt and pepper to taste, 1 teaspoon garlic powder, 1 teaspoon smoked paprika
- ✓ UK: 4 pork chops (boneless, 1-inch thick), 2 tablespoons olive oil, salt and pepper to taste, 1 teaspoon garlic powder, 1 teaspoon smoked paprika

Instructions:

1. Preheat the air fryer to 180°C (355°F).
2. Rub the pork chops with olive oil, garlic powder, smoked paprika, salt, and pepper.
3. Place the pork chops in the air fryer basket.
4. Air fry for 15-20 minutes, flipping halfway through, until the pork chops are golden and cooked through.
5. Serve with a side of your favourite keto veggies or salad.

Nutritional info: Calories: 280 | Fat: 20g | Carbs: 1g | Protein: 24g

Air Fryer Function: Air fry for juicy, tender pork chops with a nice, crispy exterior.

Keto Air Fryer Bacon-Wrapped Pork

Prep: 10 mins | Cook: 25 mins | Serves: 4

Ingredients:

- ✓ US: 500g pork tenderloin, 8 slices of bacon, 1 tablespoon olive oil, 1 teaspoon garlic powder, 1 teaspoon smoked paprika, salt and pepper to taste
- ✓ UK: 500g pork tenderloin, 8 slices of bacon, 1 tablespoon olive oil, 1 teaspoon garlic powder, 1 teaspoon smoked paprika, salt and pepper to taste

Instructions:

1. Preheat the air fryer to 200°C (390°F).
2. Rub the pork tenderloin with olive oil, garlic powder, smoked paprika, salt, and pepper.
3. Wrap the pork tenderloin with bacon slices, securing with toothpicks if necessary.
4. Place the bacon-wrapped pork in the air fryer basket.
5. Air fry for 20-25 minutes, flipping halfway through, until the bacon is crispy and the pork is cooked through.
6. Slice and serve with your favourite keto side dish.

Nutritional info: Calories: 350 | Fat: 28g | Carbs: 1g | Protein: 25g

Air Fryer Function: The air fry function crisps the bacon while keeping the pork juicy and tender.

WEEK	MONDAY	TUESDAY	WEDNESDAY	THURSDAY	FRIDAY	SATURDAY	SUNDAY
WEEK 1	Breakfast: Keto Chaffles (4 Ways) Lunch: Keto Air Fryer Chicken Fajitas Dinner: Keto Air Fryer Steak Bites	Breakfast: Keto Sausage Patties Lunch: Keto Air Fryer Cauliflower Rice (4 Ways) Dinner: Keto Air Fryer Brisket	Breakfast: Keto Breakfast Bowl (2 Ways) Lunch: Keto Air Fryer Stuffed Peppers Dinner: Keto Air Fryer Blackened Tilapia	Breakfast: Keto Cinnamon Roll Bites Lunch: Keto Air Fryer Spinach Artichoke Dip Dinner: Keto Air Fryer Pork Chops (3 Ways)	Breakfast: Keto Bacon and Egg Mini Quiches Lunch: Keto Air Fryer Brussels Sprouts Dinner: Keto Air Fryer Chicken Thighs (4 Ways)	Breakfast: Keto Air Fryer Pancakes Lunch: Keto Air Fryer Bacon-Wrapped Smokies Dinner: Keto Air Fryer Prime Rib	Breakfast: Keto Air Fryer Egg Bites (4 Ways) Lunch: Keto Mozzarella Sticks Dinner: Keto Air Fryer Lemon Pepper Cod
WEEK 2	Breakfast: Keto Breakfast Casserole Lunch: Keto Air Fryer Rouladen Dinner: Keto Air Fryer Mediterranean Veggies	Breakfast: Keto Sausage and Cheddar Muffins Lunch: Keto Air Fryer Stuffed Mushrooms Dinner: Keto Air Fryer Lemon Garlic Shrimp	Breakfast: Keto Chaffles (4 Ways) Lunch: Keto Air Fryer Cauliflower Tots Dinner: Keto Air Fryer Philly Cheesesteak	Breakfast: Keto Air Fryer Pancakes Lunch: Keto Air Fryer Zucchini Fries (3 Ways) Dinner: Keto Air Fryer Turkey Meatballs (3 Ways)	Breakfast: Keto Breakfast Tacos Lunch: Keto Air Fryer Prosciutto-Wrapped Asparagus Dinner: Keto Air Fryer Flat Iron Steak	Breakfast: Keto Egg Bites (4 Ways) Lunch: Keto Air Fryer Meatballs Dinner: Keto Air Fryer Lemon Pepper Chicken	Breakfast: Keto Chaffles Lunch: Keto Mozzarella Sticks Dinner: Keto Air Fryer Bacon-Wrapped Pork
WEEK 3	Breakfast: Keto Air Fryer Sausage Patties Lunch:	Breakfast: Keto Cinnamon Roll Bites Lunch: Keto Fried	Breakfast: Keto Breakfast Bowl Lunch: Keto Air Fryer Pesto Parmesan	Breakfast: Keto Egg Bites Lunch: Keto Fried Zucchini	Breakfast: Keto Air Fryer Bacon and Egg Cups	Breakfast: Keto Chaffles Lunch: Keto Fried Mushrooms	Breakfast: Keto Air Fryer Breakfast Tacos Lunch:

WEEK	MONDAY	TUESDAY	WEDNESDAY	THURSDAY	FRIDAY	SATURDAY	SUNDAY
	Keto Air Fryer BBQ Ribs Dinner: Keto Air Fryer Ratatouille	Green Tomatoes Dinner: Keto Air Fryer Salmon (3 Ways)	Crisps Dinner: Keto Air Fryer Chicken Drumsticks (3 Ways)	Dinner: Keto Air Fryer Garlic Butter Scallops	Lunch: Keto Air Fryer Broccoli Dinner: Keto Air Fryer Coconut Shrimp	Dinner: Keto Air Fryer Mongolian Beef	Keto Air Fryer Loaded Mashed Cauliflower Dinner: Keto Air Fryer Blackened Tilapia
WEEK 4	Breakfast: Keto Bacon and Egg Mini Quiches Lunch: Keto Air Fryer Ratatouille Dinner: Keto Air Fryer Chicken Wings	Breakfast: Keto Sausage Patties Lunch: Keto Air Fryer Brussels Sprouts Dinner: Keto Air Fryer Coconut Macaroons	Breakfast: Keto Egg Bites Lunch: Keto Air Fryer Cauliflower Wings Dinner: Keto Air Fryer Steak Bites	Breakfast: Keto Chaffles Lunch: Keto Air Fryer Asparagus (4 Ways) Dinner: Keto Air Fryer Rouladen	Breakfast: Keto Air Fryer Pancakes Lunch: Keto Buffalo Cauliflower Bites Dinner: Keto Air Fryer Prime Rib	Breakfast: Keto Cinnamon Roll Bites Lunch: Keto Air Fryer Coleslaw Dinner: Keto Air Fryer Chicken Nuggets (4 Ways)	Breakfast: Keto Chaffles (4 Ways) Lunch: Keto Air Fryer Cheese Spinach Artichoke Cups Dinner: Keto Air Fryer Philly Cheesesteak
WEEK 5	Breakfast: Keto Breakfast Bowl (2 Ways) Lunch: Keto Air Fryer Meatballs Dinner: Keto Air Fryer Lemon Pepper Cod	Breakfast: Keto Egg Bites (4 Ways) Lunch: Keto Air Fryer Stuffed Peppers Dinner: Keto Air Fryer Garlic Butter Scallops	Breakfast: Keto Sausage Patties Lunch: Keto Air Fryer Bacon Jam Dinner: Keto Air Fryer Turkey Meatballs (3 Ways)	Breakfast: Keto Cinnamon Roll Bites Lunch: Keto Fried Pickles Dinner: Keto Air Fryer Coconut Shrimp	Breakfast: Keto Chaffles Lunch: Keto Air Fryer Roasted Carrots Dinner: Keto Air Fryer Rouladen	Breakfast: Keto Bacon and Egg Mini Quiches Lunch: Keto Air Fryer Brussels Sprouts Dinner: Keto Air Fryer Prime Rib	Breakfast: Keto Sausage Patties Lunch: Keto Fried Mushrooms Dinner: Keto Air Fryer Philly Cheesesteak

WEEK	MONDAY	TUESDAY	WEDNESDAY	THURSDAY	FRIDAY	SATURDAY	SUNDAY
Week 6	Breakfast: Keto Breakfast Tacos Lunch: Keto Air Fryer Cauliflower Rice Dinner: Keto Air Fryer Chicken Wings	Breakfast: Keto Egg Bites (4 Ways) Lunch: Keto Air Fryer Bacon-Wrapped Smokies Dinner: Keto Air Fryer Salmon (3 Ways)	Breakfast: Keto Cinnamon Roll Bites Lunch: Keto Air Fryer Roasted Beets Dinner: Keto Air Fryer Lemon Garlic Shrimp	Breakfast: Keto Sausage Patties Lunch: Keto Fried Zucchini Dinner: Keto Air Fryer Coconut Macaroons	Breakfast: Keto Air Fryer Pancakes Lunch: Keto Buffalo Cauliflower Bites Dinner: Keto Air Fryer Steak Bites	Breakfast: Keto Bacon and Egg Mini Quiches Lunch: Keto Air Fryer Coleslaw Dinner: Keto Air Fryer Coconut Shrimp	Breakfast: Keto Chaffles Lunch: Keto Air Fryer Spinach Artichoke Dip Dinner: Keto Air Fryer Mongolian Beef
Week 7	Breakfast: Keto Sausage Patties Lunch: Keto Air Fryer Ratatouille Dinner: Keto Air Fryer Lemon Garlic Shrimp	Breakfast: Keto Egg Bites (4 Ways) Lunch: Keto Fried Green Tomatoes Dinner: Keto Air Fryer Prime Rib	Breakfast: Keto Cinnamon Roll Bites Lunch: Keto Air Fryer Broccoli Dinner: Keto Air Fryer Turkey Meatballs	Breakfast: Keto Breakfast Bowl (2 Ways) Lunch: Keto Air Fryer Asparagus Dinner: Keto Air Fryer Philly Cheesesteak	Breakfast: Keto Air Fryer Bacon and Egg Cups Lunch: Keto Air Fryer Zucchini Fries Dinner: Keto Air Fryer Flat Iron Steak	Breakfast: Keto Chaffles Lunch: Keto Fried Mushrooms Dinner: Keto Air Fryer Brisket	Breakfast: Keto Sausage Patties Lunch: Keto Air Fryer Mediterranean Veggies Dinner: Keto Air Fryer Garlic Butter Scallops
Week 8	Breakfast: Keto Air Fryer Pancakes Lunch: Keto Air Fryer Broccoli Dinner: Keto Air Fryer	Breakfast: Keto Chaffles (4 Ways) Lunch: Keto Fried Pickles Dinner: Keto Air Fryer Salmon	Breakfast: Keto Cinnamon Roll Bites Lunch: Keto Air Fryer Stuffed Mushrooms Dinner: Keto Air Fryer Steak Bites	Breakfast: Keto Bacon and Egg Mini Quiches Lunch: Keto Air Fryer Brussels Sprouts Dinner: Keto Air Fryer	Breakfast: Keto Sausage Patties Lunch: Keto Air Fryer Spinach Artichoke Dip Dinner:	Breakfast: Keto Chaffles Lunch: Keto Air Fryer Zucchini Fries Dinner: Keto Air Fryer Prime Rib	Breakfast: Keto Egg Bites (4 Ways) Lunch: Keto Air Fryer Coleslaw Dinner: Keto Air Fryer

WEEK	MONDAY	TUESDAY	WEDNESDAY	THURSDAY	FRIDAY	SATURDAY	SUNDAY
	Chicken Drumsticks			Lemon Pepper Cod	Keto Air Fryer Coconut Shrimp		Philly Cheesesteak

Each week provides a well-balanced variety of keto recipes from the cookbook for breakfast, lunch, and dinner using the air fryer to maximize ease and flavour. This plan keeps meals interesting, nutrient-dense, and low-carb to support a keto lifestyle.

SHOPPING LISTS

WEEKLY STAPLES

Always keep these on hand:

Proteins

- ✓ -Chicken thighs
- ✓ -Ground beef (80/20 fat ratio)
- ✓ -Eggs
- ✓ -Bacon
- ✓ -Salmon fillets

Vegetables

- ✓ -Cauliflower
- ✓ -Zucchini
- ✓ -Asparagus
- ✓ -Spinach
- ✓ -Brussels sprouts

Dairy

- ✓ -Heavy cream
- ✓ -Cream cheese
- ✓ -Shredded cheddar
- ✓ -Butter
- ✓ -Parmesan cheese

Pantry Items

- ✓ -Almond flour
- ✓ -Coconut flour
- ✓ -Pork rinds
- ✓ -Avocado oil
- ✓ -Coconut oil

Shopping by Recipe Type

Air Fryer Keto Snacks Shopping List

- ✓ -Cheese blocks for crisps
- ✓ -Zucchini
- ✓ -Seasonings (ranch, taco, Italian)

Air Fryer Keto Mains Shopping List

- ✓ -Various proteins
- ✓ -Marinades
- ✓ -Side dish ingredients

Money-Saving Tips

1. Buy in bulk when possible
2. Choose frozen vegetables when fresh are expensive
3. Watch for sales on expensive items like nuts and cheese

NUTRITIONAL INFORMATION GUIDE

UNDERSTANDING KETO MACROS

Based on my experience and consultation with nutritionists, here's a simple guide:

Standard Keto Macro Ratios

- ~70-80% calories from fat
- ~20-25% from protein
- ~5-10% from carbohydrates

How This Translates to Food

For a 2000 calorie diet:

- ~155-177g fat
- ~100-125g protein
- ~25-50g net carbs

Calculating Net Carbs

Net Carbs = Total Carbs - Fiber - Sugar Alcohols

Example Calculation:

Air Fried Zucchini (1 cup)

- ~Total Carbs: 4g
- ~Fiber: 1g
- ~Net Carbs: 3g

COMMON KETO AIR FRYER INGREDIENTS

Ingredient (100g)	Net Carbs	Fat	Protein
Chicken Thigh	0g	15g	20g
Zucchini	3g	0g	1g
Almond Flour	10g	50g	21g
Pork Rinds	0g	32g	61g

COOKING TIME CHARTS

After countless tests and timing experiments, here are my foolproof cooking times:

PROTEINS

Food Item	Temperature	Time	Notes
Chicken Wings	380°F	20-25m	Flip halfway
Salmon Fillet	400°F	7-9m	1-inch thickness
Pork Chops	375°F	12-15m	Bone-in adds 2-3 minutes
Hamburger Pat	370°F	10-12m	4oz patties

VEGETABLES

Vegetable	Temperature	Time	Notes
Asparagus	400°F	7-9m	Medium thickness
Brussels Sprout	380°F	12-15m	Halved
Cauliflower	390°F	12-14m	Bite-sized florets
Zucchini	375°F	8-10m	1/4 inch slices

KETO SNACKS

Snack Item	Temperature	Time	Notes
Cheese Crisps	360°F	5-6m	Watch closely!
Keto Chips	350°F	8-10m	Zucchini or cheese-based
Buffalo Wings	380°F	22-25m	Flip halfway

Pro Tip: Always check food 2-3 minutes before the suggested time. Air fryer models can vary!

MEASUREMENT CONVERSIONS

Temperature Conversions

Fahrenheit	Celsius
350°F	175°C
375°F	190°C
400°F	200°C

Volume Conversions

US	Metric
1 cup	240ml
1 tbsp	15ml
1 tsp	5ml

Weight Conversions

US	Metric
1 oz	28g
1 lb	454g

Common Keto Substitutions

Traditional Ingredient	Keto Substitute	Conversion Ratio
Breadcrumbs	Crushed pork rinds	1:1
Flour for breading	Almond flour	1:1
Potato wedges	Zucchini wedges	1:1

TROUBLESHOOTING GUIDE

Common Issues and Solutions

Problem: Food isn't crispy enough

Solution:

1. Pat food dry before cooking
2. Use less oil
3. Increase temperature by 25°F
4. Don't overcrowd the basket

Problem: Food is burning on the outside but raw inside

Solution:

1. Lower temperature by 25°F
2. Increase cooking time
3. Cut food into more uniform pieces

Problem: Breading falls off

Solution:

1. Pat food completely dry
2. Double-dip in egg wash
3. Let breaded food rest 5 minutes before air frying
4. Spray with oil after breading

Maintenance Tips

1. Daily Cleaning
   - ✓ -Wash removable parts after each use
   - ✓ -Wipe down exterior with damp cloth
2. Deep Cleaning (Weekly)
   - ✓ -Soak basket in hot, soapy water
   - ✓ -Clean heating element with soft brush
   - ✓ -Check for oil buildup in corners

RECIPE SCALING GUIDE

As someone who's cooked for both intimate dinners and larger gatherings, I've learned the art of scaling recipes. Here's what works:

Scaling Up

Original Amount	Double	Triple	Adjustments Needed
1 lb meat	2 lb	3 lb	Cook in batches
1 cup breading	2 cups	3 cups	None
15 min cook time	18 min	20 min	Check frequently

Scaling Down

Original Amount	Half	Quarter	Adjustments Needed
1 lb meat	1/2 lb	1/4 lb	Reduce cook time
1 cup breading	1/2 cup	1/4 cup	None
15 min cook time	12 min	10 min	Check frequently

Remember: The air fryer works best when food isn't overcrowded. Multiple batches are better than overfilling!

STORAGE AND REHEATING

Storage Guidelines

Food Type	Refrigerator	Freezer	Container Type
Cooked Meat	3-4 days	2-3 months	Airtight
Vegetables	3-5 days	8-12 months	Airtight
Cheese Crisps	5-7 days	Not recommended	Airtight

Reheating in Air Fryer

Food Type	Temperature	Time	Notes
Chicken	350°F	3-4m	Spray with oil
Vegetables	375°F	2-3m	Spread evenly
Beef	350°F	3-5m	Check center

Pro Tip: Add a spritz of oil before reheating to restore crispiness!

Remember, these are guidelines based on my experience. Your specific air fryer might require some adjustments. Don't be afraid to experiment and find what works best for you. The key to success with keto air frying is patience and practice. Keep this guide handy, and soon you'll be creating your own delicious, crispy keto meals with confidence!

CONCLUSION

As we wrap up this cookbook, I hope you're feeling inspired and confident to embark on your keto air frying adventure. When I first started combining keto cooking with air frying, I never imagined how much it would transform my approach to healthy eating. Now, after sharing my favorite recipes, techniques, and tips with you, I'm excited for you to experience the same revelation I did – that maintaining a keto lifestyle can be both delicious and convenient.

Remember, your air fryer is more than just another kitchen appliance; it's a powerful tool in your keto journey. From crispy vegetables that make you forget about carb-heavy sides, to perfectly cooked proteins that rival restaurant quality, your air fryer will help you create meals that make staying keto a joy rather than a chore.

As you've seen throughout this cookbook, the possibilities are endless. Whether you're:

- ✓ -Whipping up a quick weeknight dinner
- ✓ -Preparing meal prep basics for the week ahead
- ✓ -Creating impressive dishes for family and friends
- ✓ -Or satisfying those occasional cravings for crispy, crunchy foods

Your air fryer is there to help you do it all while staying true to your keto goals.

A Few Final Tips for Success

1. Start Simple: Begin with basic recipes and gradually work your way up to more complex dishes as your confidence grows.
2. Experiment: Don't be afraid to adapt the recipes to your taste preferences. Some of the best dishes come from creative experimentation!
3. Be Patient: Like any new cooking method, there might be a learning curve. Each air fryer model is slightly different, so take time to get to know yours.
4. Stay Inspired: Keep trying new recipes and techniques. The joy of cooking comes from continual discovery and improvement.

Beyond the Cookbook

As you continue your keto air frying journey, remember that this cookbook is just the beginning. Use it as a foundation to:

- ✓ -Develop your own signature recipes
- ✓ -Adapt family favorites to keto-friendly air fryer versions
- ✓ -Join online communities to share your successes and learn from others

The keto lifestyle is about more than just following a diet – it's about finding a sustainable way of eating that makes you feel your best. By incorporating air frying into your keto routine, you're making that lifestyle more enjoyable and achievable. Whether you're just starting your keto journey or you're a seasoned low-carb veteran, I hope this cookbook has shown you new possibilities for delicious, healthy cooking. Trust me, as someone who's been where you are, I know that with your air fryer by your side, you're well-equipped for success.

Here's to your health, happiness, and many delicious keto air fried meals ahead!

Keep cooking, stay curious, and most importantly – enjoy the journey!

Printed in Great Britain
by Amazon

57214532R00046